EXPLORING

Italian

THIRD EDITION

Joan G. Sheeran

Consultant
Marilisa Carrel Wallace

EMC
Publishing

ST. PAUL • LOS ANGELES

Developmental Editor: Jon Tremblay

Production Editor: Amy McGuire

Text Designer: Lisa Beller

Cover Designer: Leslie Anderson

Production Specialist: Parkwood Composition

Proofreader: Jen Mathe, B-books, Ltd.

Illustrations: Lachina Publishing, Rolin Graphics

Care has been taken to verify the accuracy of information presented in this book. However, the authors, editors, and publisher cannot accept responsibility for Web, e-mail, newsgroup, or chat room subject matter or content, or for consequences from application of the information in this book, and make no warranty, expressed or implied, with respect to its content.

Photo Credits

AP Photo/Bruno Luca: 180 (top left); *Calanni, Antonio:* 124 (bottom)

Bettmann/Corbis: 219 (top)

Bianchetti, Stefano/Corbis: 178 (top), 179

Bridgeman Art Library, The: 178 (bottom)

Cardinale, Stephane/People Avenue/Corbis: 180 (bottom left)

Corbis RM: 219 (bottom)

Corbis Royalty-Free: iii (bottom), 1, 13, 41 (top), 71, 76 (all), 135, 177 (top left & top right), 189 (all), 231 (top left & right, bottom right), 257 (bottom)

Desgrieux, P./photocuisine/Corbis: 113 (left)

Digital Stock: 97 (top right), 217

Digital Vision: 97 (bottom left)

Envision/Corbis: 113 (right)

Free Agents Limited/Corbis: 43 (bottom)

Guillen, J. J./epa/Corbis: 180 (top right)

iStockphoto.com: 29 (bottom left), 48, 65 (right), 85 (bottom right), 109 (bottom left & top right), 203 (bottom left), 218, 222 (top right), 257 (middle)

iStockphoto.com/Alvarez, Luis: 222 (left); *Ascione, Danilo:* 123; *Beck, Stacy:* 29 (bottom right); *Borsheim, Kelly:* 220 (left); *Braun, Michael:* 154; *Brown, Robert:* 220 (right); *Cannings-Bushell, David:* 157 (top); *Chen, Michael:* iii (right); *Cline, Kelly:* 112 (all); *Daniek, Luke:* 163 (top), 257 (top); *Gagne, Lisa:* 85 (top right); *Gjerpen, Hedda:* v, 85 (top left); *Goerg, Richard:* 109 (top left); *Gonzalex, Guillermo Perales:* 169 (top); *Habur, Izabela:* 169 (bottom); *Kindler, Björn:* iv (top); *Kopp, Sebastian:* 231 (bottom left); *Lew, Vicki:* 203 (middle); *Levstek, Tomaz:* 222 (bottom right); *Lundin, Diana:* 103 (bottom); *McNemar, Tom:* 203 (top right); *Miekuï, Peter:* 29 (top right); *Prikhodko, Viorika:* iv (bottom); *Puccio, Jack:* 109 (bottom right); *Rojo, Rey:* 65 (left); *Schenck, Timothy:* 29 (top left); *Shiyanov, Misha:* 85 (bottom left); *Tardio, Jim:* 59; *Waller, Richard:* 163 (bottom); *Weschke, Rolf:* 41 (bottom left); *van den Berg, Simone:* 103 (top)

Kraft, Wolf: 168

Mathe, David: viii (all), ix (all), 97 (bottom right), 245 (all)

Mathe, Jen: 97 (top left)

Mehlig, Manfred/zefa/Corbis: 47

National Gallery Collection, London/Corbis: 125 (bottom)

National Gallery, London/The Bridgeman Art Library: 126

PhotoEdit: x

PhotoPaq: 41 (bottom right), 44 (top), 177 (bottom), 262 (all)

Pierdomenico, Alessia/Reuters/Corbis: 180 (bottom right)

Rowell, Galen/Corbis: 45

Royse, Rachel/Corbis: 44 (bottom)

Simson, David: 157 (bottom)

Yorck Project, The: 124 (top), 125 (top), 126 (bottom)

We have made every effort to trace the ownership of all copyrighted material and to secure permission from copyright holders. In the event of any question arising as to the use of any material, we will be pleased to make the necessary corrections in future printings. Thanks are due to the aforementioned authors, publishers, and agents for permission to use the materials indicated.

ISBN 978-0-82193-489-0

Introduction

Welcome! You are entering a wonderful world filled with delicious food, delightful music, and fantastic art. A world where you can find **cool fashion** such as Prada, Gucci, Armani, Valentino, and Dolce&Gabbana; and **sporty cars** such as Alfa Romeo, Ferrari, Lamborghini, Lancia, and Maserati. All this will be accessible to you when you start speaking one of the most beautiful languages in the world—**Italian!**

Oh! One last note, if you are planning to become a famous soccer player, Italian is your language. In fact *gli Azzurri*, the Italian Soccer team, won the World Cup of Soccer four times. VIVA L' ITALIA! FORZA AZZURRI!

Italian is a Latin language, which means that it is derived from Latin just like French, Portuguese, Romanian, and Spanish. Italian is the official language in Italy and two cantons in Switzerland, the Ticino and the Grigioni. But Italian is also spoken by millions of people around the world. For example, Italian is the second most widely spoken language in Australia. This is partly due to the fact that Italians make up the largest single non-English-speaking group of migrants. Other countries with a large

number of Italian speaking people are: Malta, Monaco, Slovenia, Croatia, Argentina, Somalia, and Ethiopia.

Italian is fun to speak and it is also no trouble to read and write as the spelling is phonetic. Italian has many similarities to English in grammar and vocabulary, and many words shared between the two languages are cognates. A cognate is a word from another language that looks and/or sounds like an English word. Here are some examples of cognates: *il sistema solare, la biología, il ristorante, la musica, il telefono, il caffè, l'automobile, il mister e lo shampo*. These are all authentic Italian words that any English speaking person can immediately understand. The following are Italian words regularly used in the English language: zucchini, cinema, pasta, spaghetti, bravo, orchestra, radio, idea, and piano. See how many Italian words you already knew?

Cognates can be nouns or adjectives such as the following: *intelligente, perfetto, eccellente, favorito, sufficiente*. Recognizing these cognates will not only help you begin your study of Italian but it will help you improve your writing and speaking skills in English as well.

There is a section toward the end of each unit with symbols. Each symbol represents a word or expression in Italian. This learning method is called "Symtalk" (symbols + talking). You will be asked to "read" the sentences and then to engage in a directed dialogue with a partner or describe a scene. When you write sentences in this section, you will be talking about the characters shown below. You can refer back to this page as often as you like until you learn the names of all the characters.

Symtalk Characters

| Giuseppe | Chiara | Elisa |
| Antonio | Sara | Marco |

As you start your study of Italian, remember to be curious and ask questions. Do not be afraid to practice new sounds and sentence patterns. Someday you may use Italian in your job or when traveling, so it will have useful applications. Have fun with Italian!

Table of Contents

Exploring

Basilica di San Pietro

Molise

Salumeria

Roma

Roma

Piazza del Popolo

Villa Borghese

Campo dei Fiori

Scalinata di Trinità dei Monti

Roma

SVIZZERA

AUSTRIA

UNGHERIA

SLOVENIA

Cortina

CROAZIA

Monte Cervino ▲

Lago di Como

Piave

Lago Maggiore

Lago di Garda

BOSNIA-
ERZEGVINA

Milano

Po

Adige

Venezia

Po

Torino

Taro

FRANCIA

MARE ADRIATCO

Genova

Rapallo

A

Reno

Bologna

Rimini

MONTENEGRO

Monte Carlo

Viareggio

Arno

Firenze

San Marino

Pisa

Ombrone

P

MARE
LIGURE

ELBA

P

E

CORSICA
(FRANCIA)

Tevere

N

N

★ Roma

I

SARDEGNA

Tirso

Voltumo

N

MARE TIRRENO

Napoli

▲ Vesuvio

Alberobello

ISCHIA

Pompei

CAPRI

Agri

Taranto

MARE
MEDITERRANEO

Palermo

Belice

NERRODI

▲ Etna

MARE
IONIO

Dittaino

SICILIA

ALGERIA

TUNISIA

0   50   100 Miles

AFRICA

MALTA

0   50   100 Kilometers

X

Unit 1

I saluti e le espressioni di cortesia
Greetings and Expressions of Courtesy

Il vocabolario

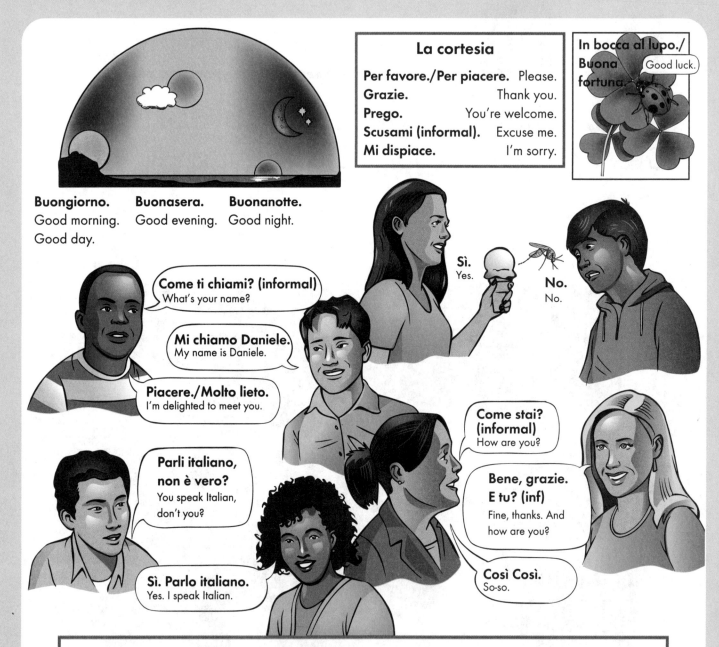

La cortesia

Per favore./Per piacere.	Please.
Grazie.	Thank you.
Prego.	You're welcome.
Scusami (informal).	Excuse me.
Mi dispiace.	I'm sorry.

In bocca al lupo./Buona fortuna. Good luck.

Buongiorno. Good morning. Good day.

Buonasera. Good evening.

Buonanotte. Good night.

Sì. Yes.

No. No.

Come ti chiami? (informal) What's your name?

Mi chiamo Daniele. My name is Daniele.

Piacere./Molto lieto. I'm delighted to meet you.

Parli italiano, non è vero? You speak Italian, don't you?

Sì. Parlo italiano. Yes. I speak Italian.

Come stai? (informal) How are you?

Bene, grazie. E tu? (inf) Fine, thanks. And how are you?

Così Così. So-so.

- When you say hello to an adult such as a teacher or a sales clerk, use the formal greeting: *Buongiorno!* and add the person's last name, if you know it, after the word *signor/signora: Buongiorno, Signor Rossi./Signora Rossi.*

- *Ciao!*, an informal and casual greeting, is usually said to a friend: *Ciao, Lina!* It is also said in taking leave from a friend: *Ciao, Lina!*

- A frequently used expression is *Piacere!* It means **it's nice to meet you./I'm pleased to meet you.**

- A woman can say *Molto lieta!* **I'm very pleased to meet you,** while a man would say *Molto lieto!*

Le lingue	Languages
il tedesco	German
l'arabo	Arabic
il cinese	Chinese
il francese	French
l'inglese	English
lo spagnolo	Spanish
il giapponese	Japanese
il portoghese	Portuguese
il russo	Russian

Vocabolario extra

Alcuni nomi di ragazze
Girls' names

Mi chiamo. . .

Anna	Marcella
Angela	Michela
Beatrice	Patrizia
Carla	Pia
Chiara	Rosa
Cristina	Sara
Diana	Stefania
Elena	Teresa
Elisabetta	Valentina
Giovanna	Vittoria
Giulia	
Isabella	**La ragazza si chiama Teresa.**
Laura	*The girl's name is Teresa.*
Maria	

Alcuni nomi di ragazzi
Boys' names

Mi chiamo. . .

Alessandro	Luigi
Alberto	Marco
Andrea	Matteo
Carlo	Nicola
Dario	Paolo
Davide	Pietro
Edoardo	Roberto
Enrico	Stefano
Fabio	Vincenzo
Franco	Vittorio
Giovanni	
Giuseppe	**Il ragazzo si chiama Carlo.**
Gregorio	*The boy's name is Carlo.*
Luca	

Le attività

A

Scegli la parola diversa dalle altre. *(Choose the word that is different from all the rest.)*

1. Ciao.	Per favore.	Prego.	Grazie.
2. Arrivederci.	Scusami.	Ci vediamo.	A domani.
3. Parli tedesco?	Come stai?	Così così.	Bene, grazie.
4. Buonasera.	Piacere.	Buongiorno.	Buonanotte.
5. Come va?	Così così.	Il giapponese.	Come stai?

B

Scegli i nomi di ragazze. *(Choose the girls' names.)*

1. Maria
2. Giovanni
3. Vittorio
4. Isabella
5. Dario
6. Patrizia
7. Luca
8. Daniele
9. Beatrice
10. Valentina

C

Rispondi alle domande in italiano. Scrivi le risposte. *(Answer the questions in Italian. Write your answers.)*

1. Parli italiano?

   _____

2. Come ti chiami?

   _____

3. Come stai?

   _____

D

Scrivi l'espressione italiana che corrisponde ad ogni immagine. *(Write the Italian expression that corresponds to each picture.)*

1. _____

2. _____

Come va?
Ciao!
Mi chiamo. . .
Grazie.
Per favore.

3. _____

4. _____

Hello!
Please.
Excuse me.
Yes.
Thank you.

5. _____

6. _____

7. _____

E **Scrivi delle risposte brevi in italiano.** *(Short answers.)*

1. How do you greet someone in the morning?

   _____

2. How do you greet someone in the evening?

   _____

3. What is customary to say after meeting someone?

   _____

4. How do you wish someone good luck?

   _____

5. Finish the following sentence:

   Io parlo _____.

6. *Ciao!*, an informal greeting, would generally be used to greet: _____

   A. a friend, Roberto   or   B. a gentleman, *il signor Zini*

7. Is Michela a name for a *ragazzo*?

   _____

8. Answer this question: *Come ti chiami?*

   _____

9. One word for farewell is _____.

10. *Sì* is the opposite of _____.

F **Completa il dialogo in italiano. Scrivi le tue risposte.** (*Complete the dialogue in Italian. Write your answers.*)

1. MARIA: Ciao! Mi chiamo Maria, e tu?

   GIACOMO: _____

2. LORENZO: Come stai, Rosa?

   ROSA: Bene, grazie. _____

3. SARA: Parli italiano?

   GIORGIO: Sì, _____

G **Parliamo!** **Talk with a classmate but pretend to meet for the first time. Act out a simple introduction.**

H **Tocca a te!** (*It's your turn!*) **Che cosa sai dire in italiano?** (*What can you say in Italian?*)

1. Shake hands as you say hello to a friend.

2. Wave and say good-bye to a friend.

3. Name at least five boys' names and five girls' names.

4. Say that you speak English.

Proverbio

" **Cortesia di bocca assai vale e poco costa.** Courtesy costs little and is worth a lot. "

Lingua viva!

FELICITAZIONI!

Auguri a...

Grazie

Benvenuti a San Pietro

referente fuori regione per contatti in caso di emergenza	
nome/cognome	
indirizzo	
telefoni	
cellulare	
posta elettronica	

Cari Amici Buon Natale!

I   **Look at these clippings and find the following words in Italian.**

1. Welcome

   _____

2. Merry Christmas

   _____

3. Thank you

   _____

4. Congratulations

   _____

5. Best Wishes to . . .

   _____

J   **This emergency card requires certain information. Guess the English meaning of the following words.**

1. Nome

   _____

2. Cognome

   _____

3. Indirizzo

   _____

4. Telefono

   _____

5. Cellulare

   _____

6. Posta elettronica

   _____

Symtalk

K Scrivi nello spazio la parola giusta in italiano. *(In the space, write the correct word in Italian.)*

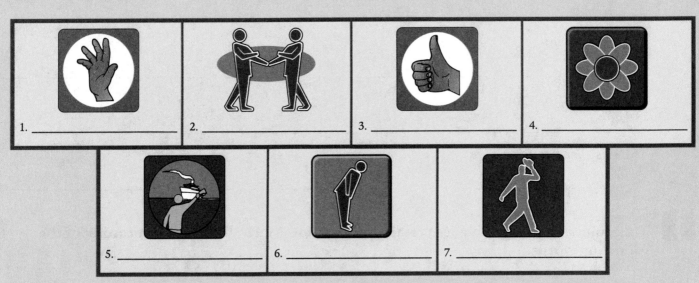

1. _____

2. _____

3. _____

4. _____

5. _____

6. _____

7. _____

L Dì le frasi, poi scrivile in italiano. *(Say the sentences, then write them in Italian.)*

1. _____

2. _____

3. _____

4. _____

Guarda i simboli, poi scrivi i dialoghi in italiano. (*Look at the symbols, then write the dialogues.*)

1. _____

_____

_____

2. _____

_____

3. _____

_____

Il cruciverba

Orizzontale

3. Mi ____ Gianluca.
4. Ci ____. *(See you later.)*
5. I'm sorry, in Italian. *Mi* ____.
10. E ____?
11. *per favore*, in English
12. opposite of *no*
13. Good-bye, in Italian (informal)

Verticale

1. ____ stai?
2. A ____. *(See you tomorrow.)*
3. informal greeting
6. ____. *(I'm pleased to meet you.)*
7. courtesy
8. Laura says "*molto* ____" after she meets Carlo.
9. Come ____? *(How are you?)*

Unit 2

Gli oggetti e i comandi dell'aula
Classroom Objects and Commands

Il vocabolario

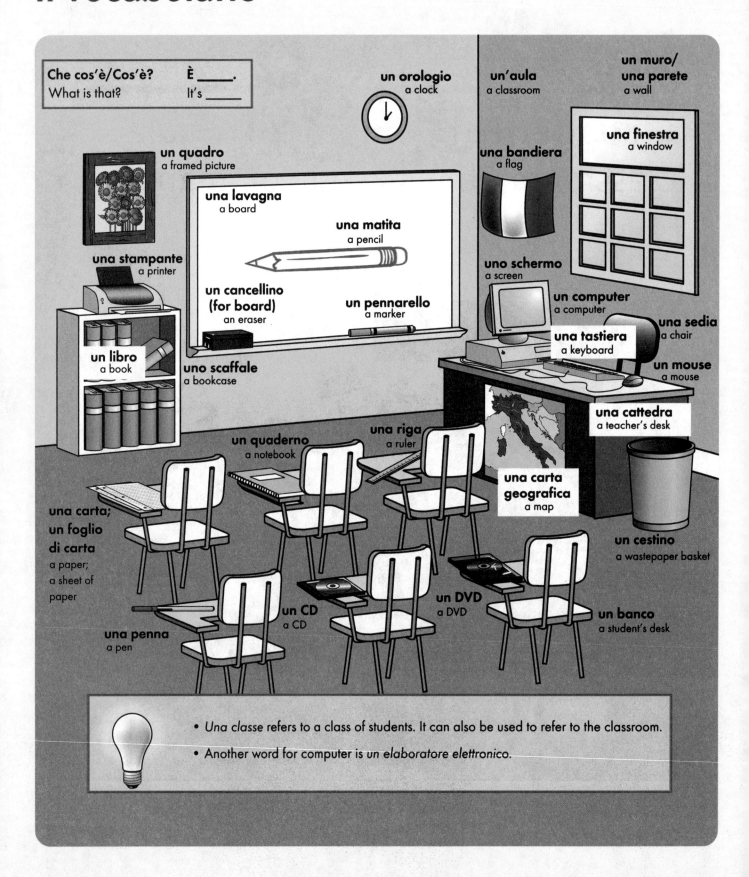

Che cos'è/Cos'è? È _____.
What is that? It's _____

un orologio
a clock

un'aula
a classroom

un muro/
una parete
a wall

una bandiera
a flag

una finestra
a window

un quadro
a framed picture

una lavagna
a board

una matita
a pencil

uno schermo
a screen

un computer
a computer

una sedia
a chair

una stampante
a printer

un cancellino
(for board)
an eraser

un pennarello
a marker

una tastiera
a keyboard

un mouse
a mouse

un libro
a book

uno scaffale
a bookcase

una cattedra
a teacher's desk

un quaderno
a notebook

una riga
a ruler

una carta
geografica
a map

una carta;
un foglio
di carta
a paper;
a sheet of
paper

un cestino
a wastepaper basket

un CD
a CD

un DVD
a DVD

un banco
a student's desk

una penna
a pen

• *Una classe* refers to a class of students. It can also be used to refer to the classroom.

• Another word for computer is *un elaboratore elettronico*.

I comandi dell'aula
Classroom commands

Dillo in italiano.
Say it in Italian.

Parla.
Speak.

Ripeti.
Repeat.

Vai/Và alla lavagna.
Go to the board.

Scrivi.
Write.

Rispondi alla domanda.
Answer the question.

Alza la mano.
Raise your hand.

Prendi un foglio di carta.
Take out a sheet of paper.

Apri il libro.
Open the book.

Chiudi il libro.
Close the book.

Leggi.
Read.

Ascolta.
Listen.

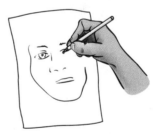

Fai/Fà uno schizzo (un disegno, un'illustrazione).
Make a sketch (drawing, illustration).

Completa le frasi.
Complete the sentences.

Accendi il computer.
Turn the computer on.

Spegni il computer.
Turn the computer off.

Vocabolario extra

mandare un fax *to send a fax*	**navigare in Internet** *to surf the Web, (the Net)*	**copiare** *to copy*
mandare/spedire un e-mail; mandare/ spedire una posta elettronica *to send an e-mail*	**stampare** *to print*	**giocare ad un videogioco** *to play a video game*

Le attività

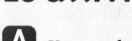

Your teacher will say at random the words for 26 classroom objects. After you hear the first word, find it in the list below and write "1" in the space provided. The second word you hear will be marked "2," etc.

_____ una lavagna	_____ un foglio di carta
_____ una riga	_____ un pennarello
_____ un CD	_____ una matita
_____ una penna	_____ un quaderno
_____ un libro	_____ un mouse
_____ una carta geografica	_____ un orologio
_____ un cestino	_____ uno scaffale
_____ una stampante	_____ una gomma
_____ una bandiera	_____ una finestra
_____ una tastiera	_____ uno schermo
_____ un quadro	_____ un banco
_____ una sedia	_____ una cattedra
_____ un computer	_____ un DVD

B **Look around your own classroom as you answer these questions.**

1. Do you have *un foglio di carta* on your desk?

   _____

2. Where is the *bandiera*?

   _____

3. How many *finestre* does your room have?

_____

4. Is the *stampante* near the computer?

_____

5. Are there many *libri* in the *scaffale?*

_____

 Scrivi il nome di ogni oggetto in italiano. *(Write the Italian name for each object. Don't forget to write the indefinite article* **un, uno, un'** *or* **una** *before the noun.)*

1. _____

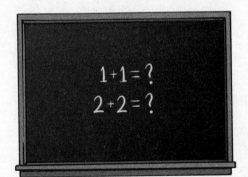

2. _____

3. _____

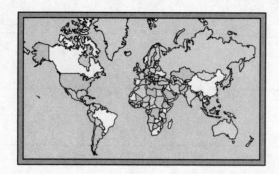

4. _____

5. _____

6. _____

7. _____

Gli oggetti e i comandi dell'aula

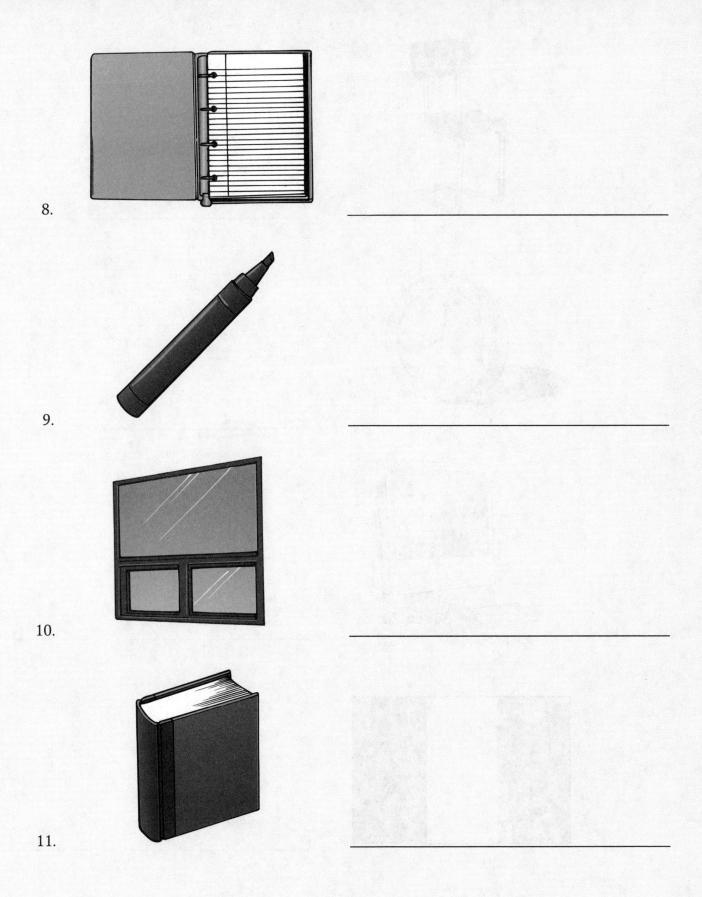

8. _____

9. _____

10. _____

11. _____

12. _____

13. _____

14. _____

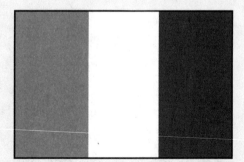

15. _____

D Completa le frasi. *(Complete the sentences.)*

1. _____ è?

2. _____ una penna.

3. È _____ sedia.

4. È _____ libro.

E Do what your teacher commands.

F Completa i comandi in italiano. *(Please complete the commands in Italian.)*

1. _____ inglese. *(speak)*

2. _____ in inglese. *(say it)*

3. _____. *(listen)*

4. _____ il computer. *(turn off)*

5. _____ il libro. *(open)*

G Completa le frasi in italiano. *(Complete the sentences in Italian.)*

1. Prendi un foglio di _____.

2. Ripeti le _____.

3. Chiudi il _____.

4. Fai un _____.

5. Accendi il _____.

6. Scrivi con una _____.

7. Rispondi alla _____.

H Scrivi un comando in italiano per ogni disegno. *(Write a command in Italian for each illustration.)*

1. _____

2.  _____

3.  _____

4.  _____

5.  _____

I Which objects go together? Match each noun in column *A* with a related noun in column *B*.

A	B
1. _____ un mouse	A. una parete
2. _____ una cattedra	B. uno schermo
3. _____ un pennarello	C. un quaderno
4. _____ un foglio di carta	D. una lavagna
5. _____ un quadro	E. una sedia

J Parliamo! Point to a classroom object, such as a ruler. Ask: *"È una riga?"* Your partner should answer, *"Sì, è una riga."* Point to a window. Ask: *"È una matita?"* Your partner should answer, *"No, è una finestra."* Find ten items.

K Word associations. You and your speaking partner should each make a list of five words from the classroom commands. Ask each other to say anything related to that word.

Modello:	A: la mano
	B: alza
	or
	B: dillo
	A: in italiano

L Tocca a te! With a partner walk around your classroom, pointing to ten different objects. Ask your partner *"Che cos'è?"* If he/she answers incorrectly, change places. Now it is his/her turn to ask you the name of each item. Keep going until all ten objects have been correctly identified.

Matite colorate
€3,50

strumenti di scrittura
BIC
O-KAY AD
Bellissime penne
€1,00

€23,00

Zainetto per la scuola
Disegni assortiti e in tinta unica
giallo, rosso, e verde

CARTOLIBRERIA
BERGAMINO M. L.
VIA CHANOUX, 96
CHATILLON (AO)
P.IVA: 00122670078

REPARTO 1   EURO
                    1.10

TOTALE €   1.10

14-08-2006 15:26 SC 14

TEL. 0166/61806

NF CM 13701262

Look at the clippings and find the following information.

1. What do you think *cartolibreria* means?

_____

2. Find the Italian words for "colored pencils."

_____

3. How much does one packet of colored pencils cost?

_____

4. Find the Italian word for "pens."

_____

5. How much do you have to pay to buy one pen?

_____

 Look at the backpack ad and find the following information.

1. Find the word for "backpack" in Italian.

_____

2. What does the word *scuola* mean?

_____

3. Is *scuola* a masculine or a feminine noun?

_____

4. What do you think *disegni assortiti* means?

_____

5. The backpack is also offered in three solid colors, which ones?

_____

Proverbio

" Bisogna prima pensare, poi fare. Look before you leap. **"**

Symtalk

O Scrivi nello spazio la parola giusta in italiano. *(In the space, write the correct word in Italian.)*

1. _____
2. _____
3. _____
4. _____
5. _____
6. _____
7. _____
8. _____
9. _____
10. _____

P Dì le frasi, poi scrivile in italiano. *(Say the sentences, then write them in Italian.)*

1.

2.

3.

4.

_____

Q **Scrivi una descrizione di ogni scena in italiano.** *(Write a description of each scene in Italian.)*

1.

_____
_____
_____
_____

2.

_____
_____
_____
_____

3.

_____
_____
_____
_____

Il cruciverba

Orizzontale

1. large desk
5. _____ della classe (*classroom objects*)
9. Write.
10. storage place for books: _____.
11. used to erase the board
12. _____ alla lavagna. (*Go the board.*)

Verticale

1. small round disk used in the computer
2. _____ la finestra. (*Open the window.*)
3. opening in a wall for air and light
4. printing machine
6. _____ della classe (*classroom commands*)
7. viewing screen
8. _____ alla domanda. (*Answer the question.*)

Unit 3

I numeri

Numbers

Il vocabolario

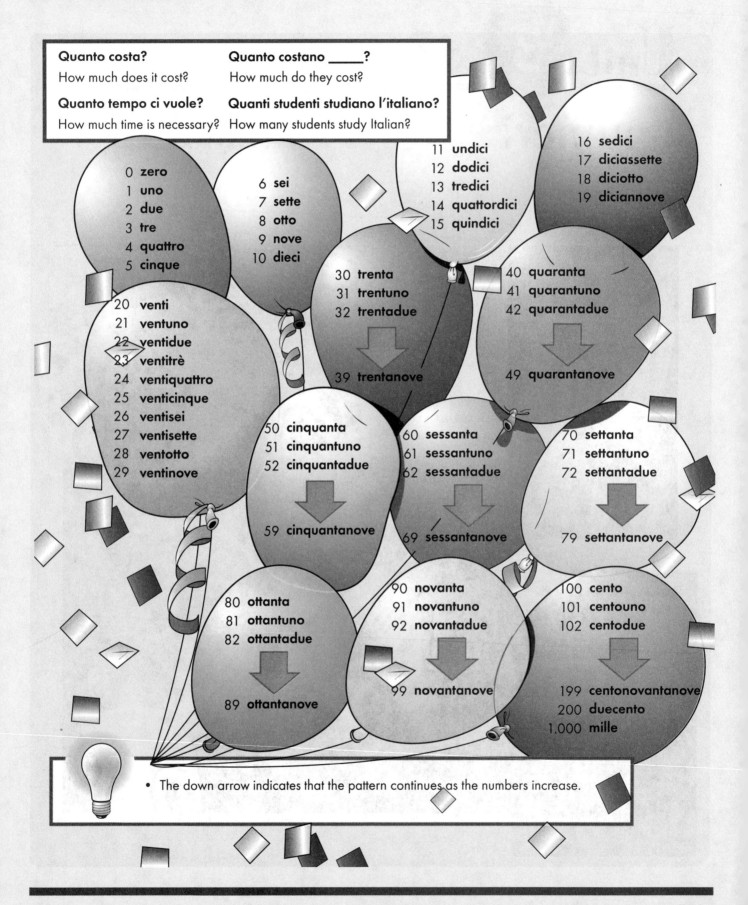

Quanto costa?
How much does it cost?

Quanto costano _____?
How much do they cost?

Quanto tempo ci vuole?
How much time is necessary?

Quanti studenti studiano l'italiano?
How many students study Italian?

0	zero
1	uno
2	due
3	tre
4	quattro
5	cinque

6	sei
7	sette
8	otto
9	nove
10	dieci

11	undici
12	dodici
13	tredici
14	quattordici
15	quindici

16	sedici
17	diciassette
18	diciotto
19	diciannove

20	venti
21	ventuno
22	ventidue
23	ventitrè
24	ventiquattro
25	venticinque
26	ventisei
27	ventisette
28	ventotto
29	ventinove

30	trenta
31	trentuno
32	trentadue
↓	
39	trentanove

40	quaranta
41	quarantuno
42	quarantadue
↓	
49	quarantanove

50	cinquanta
51	cinquantuno
52	cinquantadue
↓	
59	cinquantanove

60	sessanta
61	sessantuno
62	sessantadue
↓	
69	sessantanove

70	settanta
71	settantuno
72	settantadue
↓	
79	settantanove

80	ottanta
81	ottantuno
82	ottantadue
↓	
89	ottantanove

90	novanta
91	novantuno
92	novantadue
↓	
99	novantanove

100	cento
101	centouno
102	centodue
↓	
199	centonovantanove
200	duecento
1.000	mille

• The down arrow indicates that the pattern continues as the numbers increase.

Vocabolario extra

Quanto/Quanta?
How much?

Quanti/Quante?
How many?

Ci sono? C'è?
Are there? Is there?

Quanto costa il libro?
How much does the book cost?

Il libro costa dieci dollari.
The book costs ten dollars.

Quanti quaderni ci sono?
How many notebooks are there?

Ce ne sono cinque.
There are five.

Quanto fa due più uno?
How much is two plus one?

Fa tre.
That equals three.

costare	
to cost	
costa	**costano**
(it) costs	*(they) cost*

$+$ = *più* $\times$ = *per* $-$ = *meno* $\div$ = *diviso*

Le attività

A After you have studied the numbers and practiced saying them, try to write the numbers below from memory. *In italiano, per favore.*

1. _____   6. _____

2. _____   7. _____

3. _____   8. _____

4. _____   9. _____

5. _____   10. _____

B Rate yourself. How did you do? Circle your evaluation.

1. very well   2. fairly well   3. poorly

C Practice again. Identify the words by writing the corresponding Arabic numerals.

> **Modello:** due ___2___

1. cinque _____   4. nove _____

2. otto _____   5. sette _____

3. uno _____

D Scrivi la parola italiana per ogni numero. *(Write the Italian word for each number.)*

1. (3) _____   3. (6) _____

2. (4) _____   4. (10) _____

E Tell whether the following equations indicate addition, subtraction, multiplication, or division.

1. Quattordici diviso sette fa due.

_____

2. Due più dieci fa dodici.

_____

3. Otto per tre fa ventiquattro.

_____

4. Diciannove meno tredici fa sei.

_____

F Try once more to write out the Italian words for the following numbers. *In italiano, per favore.*

1. (8) _____   6. (2) _____

2. (3) _____   7. (5) _____

3. (10) _____   8. (4) _____

4. (1) _____   9. (7) _____

5. (9) _____   10. (6) _____

G Quanti oggetti ci sono in ogni gruppo? *(How many objects are pictured in each group?)* Write out the Italian numbers. Do not use numerals!

1. _____

2. _____

3. _____

4. _____

5. _____

H **Quanti oggetti ci sono in totale?** *(How many objects are there all together?)* _____

Now, write this sum in Italian.

_____

I Scrivi le risposte in italiano. *(Write the answers in Italian.)*

> **Modello:** 6 − 4 = __due__

1. 12 × 4 = _____
2. 30 − 10 = _____
3. 8 − 6 = _____
4. 12 + 18 = _____
5. 100 ÷ 2 = _____

6. 60 + 10 = _____
7. 30 − 15 = _____
8. 80 ÷ 2 = _____
9. 10 × 10 = _____
10. 15 + 4 = _____

J Your teacher will say ten numbers in Italian. Write the corresponding Arabic numerals.

> **Modello:** Teacher says: diciannove
> You write: __19__

1. _____
2. _____
3. _____
4. _____
5. _____

6. _____
7. _____
8. _____
9. _____
10. _____

K How many interior angles are there in each design? Circle the number.

1.

quattro   dieci

otto   tre

3.

sette   undici

sei   cinque

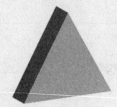

2.

cinque   quattro

tre   sette

4.

cinque   otto

nove   undici

Leggi il paragrafo. Poi, scegli le risposte corrette. (*Read the paragraph. Then choose the correct completions and answers.*)

> Nell'aula ci sono molti oggetti. Ci sono ventotto sedie, quattro finestre, diciannove quaderni, sei cancellini e una carta geografica. Una sedia costa settantuno dollari. Una gomma costa novanta centesimi e una carta geografica costa ottanta dollari.

dollari dollars · **centesimi** cents

1. Nell'aula ci sono __ oggetti.
   A. pochi (*few*)
   B. molti
   C. mille
   D. tre

2. In totale, ci sono __ oggetti dell'aula. (*Add.*)
   A. quarantuno
   B. cinquantotto
   C. ventidue
   D. novanta

3. Quanto costa una sedia?
   A. $75
   B. $57
   C. $37
   D. $71

4. Quanti quaderni ci sono?
   A. 91
   B. 25
   C. 19
   D. 30

5. Quante finestre ci sono?
   A. 13
   B. 8
   C. 6
   D. 4

M **Parliamo! Find out about prices. With your speaking partner, select six objects in the classroom. You ask how much each of the first three objects costs. Then your partner should ask you about the remaining three items and you will answer.**

> **Modello:** **A:** Quanto costa la penna? (*How much does the pen cost?*)
> **B:** Costa due dollari. (*It costs two dollars.*)

N **Tocca a te! With a classmate find out how many things are in your classroom. Look for these items: *libri* (books), *finestre* (windows), *quaderni* (notebooks), *penne* (pens), *computer* (computers), and *banchi* (student desks). After you have counted carefully, announce your findings to the class. At the end, add all of the items to find out the total number of things you have. Write all numbers on your classroom board.**

> **Modello:** **A:** Quanti libri ci sono? (*How many books are there?*)
> **B:** Ci sono venti libri. (*There are twenty books.*)

1	COME SIAMO TANTI AL MONDO - Biagio Antonacci	MQRS141 P	MQRS141
2	COSI' PRESTO NO - Biagio Antonacci	MQRS142 P	MQRS142
3	IRIS - Biagio Antonacci	MQRS143 P	MQRS143
4	LASCIAMI ANDARE VIA - Biagio Antonacci	MQRS144 P	MQRS144
5	LIBERATEMI - Biagio Antonacci	MQRS145 P	MQRS145
6	NON PARLI MAI - Biagio Antonacci	MQRS146 P	MQRS146
7	NON SO PIU' A CHI CREDERE - Biagio Antonacci	MQRS147 P	MQRS147
8	SE E' VERO CHE CI SEI - Biagio Antonacci	MQRS148 P	MQRS148
9	BUFFALO SOLDIER - Bob Marley	MQRS149 P	MQRS149
10	COULD YOU BE LOVED - Bob Marley	MQRS150 P	MQRS150
11	DON'T TURN AROUND - Bob Marley	MQRS151 P	MQRS151
12	EXODUS - Bob Marley	MQRS152 P	MQRS152
13	GET UP STAND UP - Bob Marley	MQRS153 P	MQRS153
14	I SHOT THE SHERIFF - Bob Marley	MQRS154 P	MQRS154
15	IS THIS LOVE - Bob Marley	MQRS155 P	MQRS155
16	ONE LOVE PEOPLE GET READY - Bob Marley	MQRS156 P	MQRS156
17	REDEMPTION SONG - Bob Marley	MQRS157 P	MQRS157
18	REGGAE FEVER - Bob Marley	MQRS158 P	MQRS158
19	SATISFY MY SOUL - Bob Marley	MQRS159 P	MQRS159
20	STIR IT UP - Bob Marley	MQRS160 P	MQRS160

Stazione Centrale

PIAZZA MEDAGLIE D'ORO
STAZIONE FS

Piazza Medaglie D'oro

Viale Pietramellara

BONOMELLI

Camomilla
solubile
"Bonomelli"
scatola da 100 g.
16 + 4 bustine
omaggio (**)
€ 1,35
€ 0,94

brioss

€ 1,45
€ 1,01

10 Merendine
brioss "Ferrero"
280 g, ciliegia / albicocca

il tuo NEWS

14/2006
offerta valida
dal 10 al 22 luglio 2006

O   **Look at the list of songs then write out, in Italian, the numbers by each of the following songs:**

1. Exodus _____

2. Così presto no _____

3. Liberatemi _____

4. Is this love _____

5. Lasciami andare via _____

P   **Look at the other clippings and find the following information. Please write the numbers in Italian.**

1. How many BRIOSS are in one package?

   _____

2. How many *bustine* (tea bags) do you get when you buy a box of Camomilla Bonomelli?

   _____

3. *Stazione Centrale* is the central train station. How many stops numbered *trentasei* can you find in the clipping?

   _____

4. What is the number for the **red** train stop?

   _____

5. What is the train stop with the highest number?

   _____

Proverbio

" **Quattro occhi vedono meglio di due.**
Two heads are better than one. "

Symtalk

Q Scrivi nello spazio la parola giusta in italiano. *(In the space, write the correct word in Italian.)*

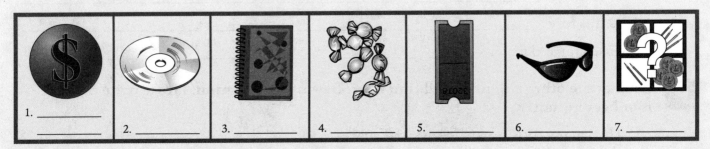

1. _____   2. _____   3. _____   4. _____   5. _____   6. _____   7. _____

R Dì le frasi, poi scrivile in italiano. *(Say the sentences, then write them in Italian.)*

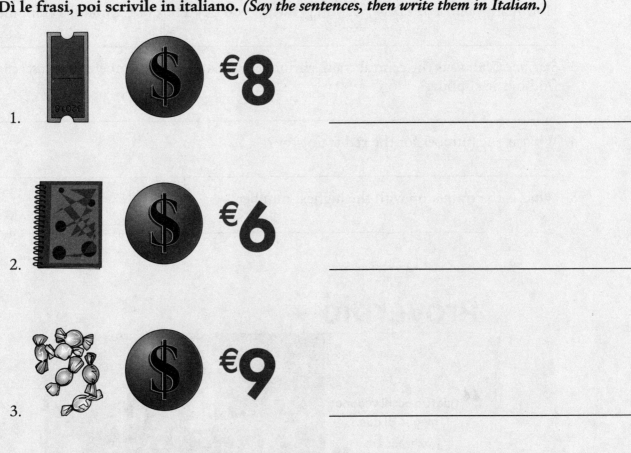

1. €8 _____

2. €6 _____

3. €9 _____

4. €24 _____

S Quanto costa ogni oggetto? Con un compagno, fate le domande, rispondete e scrivetele in un dialogo. *(How much does each item cost? With a partner, ask the question or give the answer. Then write the dialogue.)*

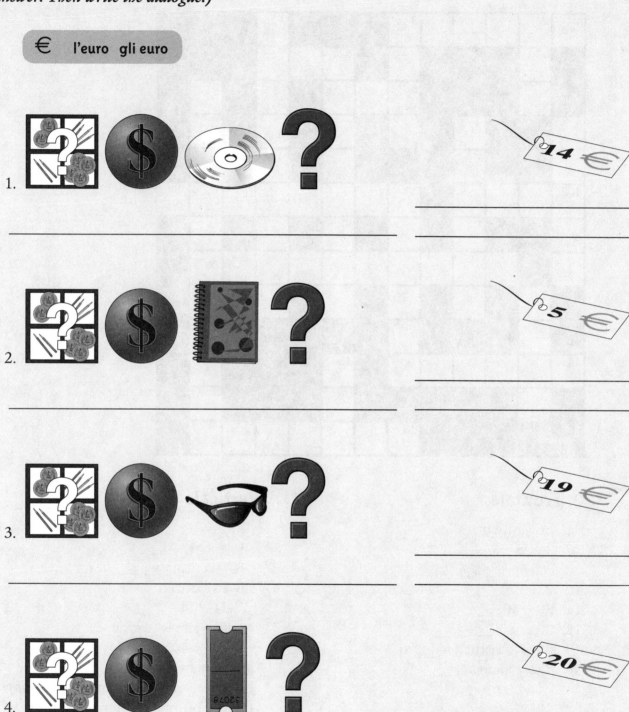

€ l'euro gli euro

1.

_____

14 €

_____

2.

_____

5 €

_____

3.

_____

19 €

_____

4.

_____

20 €

_____

Il cruciverba

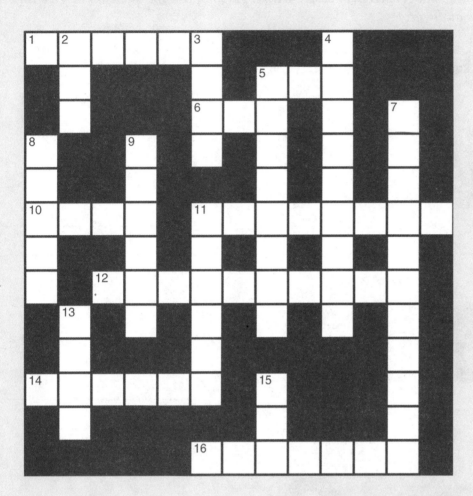

Orizzontale

1. how much
5. $2 \times 3 =$ _____
6. *otto meno cinque fa* _____
10. $7 + 2 =$ _____
11. $50 - 10 =$ _____
12. $80 + 8 =$ _____
14. one fewer than a dozen
16. *dodici più uno fa* _____

Verticale

2. $1 - 0 =$ _____
3. $4 + 4 =$ _____
4. ½ century = _____ years
5. five dozen
7. $56 \div 4 =$ _____
8. five times twenty
9. $70 - 40 =$ _____
11. how many
13. name of the sign indicating subtraction
15. the number of items in a pair

Unit 4

La geografia   Geography

Italia

Ten Important cities

Roma (Rome), the nation's capital, is located on the Tiber River. Because of its long history, Roma is often called "The Eternal City." Among its ancient ruins are the Colosseum, an amphitheater or stadium; the Roman Forum, a public area once surrounded by temples and governmental buildings; and the Pantheon, a Greek-style temple devoted to all the gods in the former Roman religion.

Today the city attracts many visitors to its works of art, churches, squares, and fountains. Within the city limits is the independent papal state of the Vatican, the headquarters of the Roman Catholic Church.

Firenze (Florence) is a Tuscan city on the Arno River most closely associated with the treasures of the Renaissance, such as the statue of *David* by Michelangelo. It also has two famous bell towers. The older one, part of the Palazzo Vecchio, is decorated at the top with coats of arms. The newer one, designed by the Renaissance painter and architect Giotto, is part of the cathedral complex. It has beautiful carvings and designs on the outside. Nearby is another cultural landmark: three sets of large, decorated bronze doors.

The Roman Forum in Roma

Milano (Milan) is the manufacturing center and capital of the northern region of Lombardy. It is known as a leader in textiles, fashion design, and banking. It is also the home of the world famous opera house, La Scala. Leonardo da Vinci's *fresco* (wall painting) *The Last Supper* is centrally located in the city. There is a museum of science and technology named after this artist, who was also a scientist and an inventor.

Genova (Genoa) is the hilly capital of the northern region of Liguria, and the largest seaport of Italy. It is the city commonly believed to be the birthplace of Cristoforo Colombo. It is also the city in which the imprisoned Marco Polo dictated the stories of his adventures.

Torino (Turin) is a major industrial city situated on the Po River. It manufactures automobiles, such as Fiat and Alfa Romeo, as well as buses, tires, and clothing. It was the site of the 2006 winter Olympics.

La Scala in Milano

Venezia (Venice) is the island city of medieval streets and canals. Located on the Adriatic Sea, Venice does not allow automobiles within its boundaries. It has three major sites: the Basilica of Saint Mark, an elaborately decorated church; the Palace of the Doge (former ruler); and the Grand Canal itself, the subject of many paintings by the artist Canaletto. Venice is a glass-making center, making vases, chandeliers, drinking glasses, and jewelry.

Gondolas in Venezia

Napoli (Naples) is a southwestern industrial city overlooking a large bay. It is Italy's second largest port and headquarters of the airline Alitalia. Both children and adults enjoy visiting the National Archeological Museum where they can learn about the country's antiquities. They can also see a medieval castle, a seventeenth-century palace, and a modern aquarium. A visit of the city is not complete without trying the delicious Neapolitan ice cream.

Siracusa (Syracuse) is a city on the eastern shore of Sicily. Originally part of the ancient Greek empire, Siracusa honors its past with performances of plays in Greek in the old Greek theater. It has a Roman amphitheater as well.

Palermo is the capital of Sicily. Having both a Phoenician and a Viking (Norse) history, Palermo is the largest port on the island. After an all night ride in a ferry boat from Naples, visitors usually plan a stop at the Palace of the Normans. Mosaics found here are some of the most beautiful in Europe.

Cagliari is the capital and major city on the island of Sardegna (Sardinia). Visitors can enjoy the new seaside resort and admire the flowers in the botanical gardens. Cagliari, too, has a Roman ampitheater.

Palazzo dei Normanni (Palace of the Normans)

Important Facts

- Italy is a boot-shaped South European country extending into the Mediterranean Sea. The north is heavily industrial, manufacturing many products such as office equipment, cars, and clothing. The south is generally agricultural, producing olives, grapes, and other fruits and vegetables. Italy is divided into twenty regions, each with its own traditions, dialect, and unique characteristics.

- The Alps stretch across the northern borders with France, Switzerland, Austria, and Slovenia. The Alps include some of the highest peaks in Europe and they are a favorite destination for skiers in winter as well as mountain climbers in the summer.

- The Apennine Mountain Range extends vertically throughout most of the country. It begins as hills near Genova and stretches all the way to the southern regions.

Town of Riomaggiore in the Italian Riviera

- The pleasant coastal area from the French border to Genova is called "The Italian Riviera." It attracts many vacationers.

- The Po River Valley is a large fertile area with an excellent system of transportation (both rail and highway) and much agriculture and industry.

- The Adriatic coast has two cities of great contrast: Rimini, a modern beach resort, and Brindisi, a seaport and end point of the Appian Way, the ancient road from Roma.

- *La Sicilia* (Sicily) and *La Sardegna* (Sardinia) are the two largest Italian islands. With their unique vegetation, white and coral sandy beaches, and clear blue water, they are a favorite destination for tourists. Inland local people are still largely farmers and sheep ranchers.

Names
il Mare Mediterraneo = Mediterranean Sea
il Mare Ligure = Liguran Sea
il Mare Tirreno = Tyrrhenian Sea
il Mare Ionio = Ionian Sea
il Mare Adriatico = Adriatic Sea
Le Alpi = the Alps
Gli Appennini = the Apennines

Two of the most famous Italian volcanoes are Mount Vesuvius *(Vesuvio)* south of Naples and Mount Etna on the island of Sicily.

Le attività

Write the letter of each city on the map next to its name below.

1. _____ Genova

2. _____ Palermo

3. _____ Napoli

4. _____ Roma

5. _____ Venezia

6. _____ Milano

7. _____ Cagliari

8. _____ Torino

9. _____ Siracusa

10. _____ Firenze

B Identify the cities described in the information below.

1. popular beach resort on the Adriatic coast

   _____

2. site of the Vatican

   _____

3. site of Greek and Roman ruins

   _____

4. industrial city overlooking a large bay

   _____

5. center of glass making

   _____

6. capital of Sicilia

   _____

7. home of Cristoforo Colombo

   _____

8. city of art

   _____

9. center of automotive industry

   _____

10. center of fashion and banking

   _____

Seaside town of Castellammare del Golfo in Sicilia

Study the map of Italy carefully. Then find the following items and write down your answer.

1. two mountain ranges

   _____

2. two islands

   _____

3. two seaports

   _____

4. four seas within the Mediterranean

   _____

   _____

The Leaning Tower of Pisa
(Torre pendente di Pisa)

D Match Column *A* with Column *B*.

	A		B
1. _____	Pantheon	A.	a nickname for Roma
2. _____	Colosseum	B.	Giotto's gift to Firenze
3. _____	bell tower	C.	located in Venezia
4. _____	Appian Way	D.	statue in Firenze
5. _____	the Apennines	E.	horizontal mountain range
6. _____	the Alps	F.	ancient ruin in Roma
7. _____	*David*	G.	ancient road
8. _____	The Grand Canal	H.	Roman temple built in Greek style
9. _____	La Scala	I.	vertical mountain range
10. _____	"The Eternal City"	J.	opera house

E Nomina la città associata con ciascun' immagine. *(Name the city associated with each illustration.)*

1. _____

2. _____

3. _____

4. _____

5. _____

F **Completa correttamente ogni frase.** *(Complete the sentences.)*

1. *Sardegna* is a(n) _____.
   A. island
   B. mountain
   C. river
   D. city

2. *Italia* is geographically shaped like a _____.
   A. glove
   B. shoe
   C. hat
   D. boot

3. *Rimini* is a _____.
   A. ski area
   B. beach resort
   C. port
   D. industrial center

4. The *Arno* is a _____.
   A. city
   B. volcano
   C. river
   D. glacier

5. The statue of *David* by Michelangelo is found in _____.
   A. Firenze
   B. Genova
   C. Napoli
   D. Siracusa

6. The wall painting entitled *The Last Supper* is found in _____.
   A. Torino
   B. Milano
   C. Venezia
   D. Palermo

7. Mount Etna is an active volcano on the island of _____.
   A. Elba
   B. Sicilia
   C. Capri
   D. Sardegna

8. Italy can be described best as _____.
   A. swampy
   B. flat
   C. mountainous
   D. sandy

9. Southeastern Italy is generally _____.
   A. industrial
   B. artistic
   C. agricultural
   D. thickly populated

10. On Sardegna, the city of Cagliari is located in the _____.
    A. south
    B. west
    C. north
    D. east

G **Write in each blank space the answer that makes each statement geographically correct.**

Italy's neighbors are Switzerland, France, Slovenia, and (1) _____. The
European mountain range of the (2) _____ extends through north-central
Italy. The (3) _____ River flows from the north through Roma,
(4) _____, emptying into the (5) _____ Sea. The city of
Venezia is located on one large (6) _____ and several smaller ones. Genova,
lying at the foothills of the (7) _____ Mountain Range, is very hilly. The city
of Napoli is situated on the large bay overlooking the (8) _____ Sea. The
Adriatic coast has two cities of great contrast: Rimini and (9) _____, the end
point of the Appian Way. Italy's largest islands are called (10) _____
and (11) _____.

H Imagine that you must plan an itinerary (list of sightseeing places) for a group of American tourists. The first group would like to see cultural sites (i.e., things pertaining to music, art, theater, and civilization). The second group would like to visit recreational areas for winter or summer activities. Which places would you recommend for each group?

Group 1 _____

_____

_____

_____

_____

Group 2 _____

_____

_____

_____

_____

I Name three places you would like to visit if you were the winner of a three-week vacation in Italy. (You get to choose the season.) Tell why you selected these places. What would you see or do there?

_____

_____

_____

_____

_____

_____

_____

_____

_____

_____

_____

_____

J Maze. Laura and Paolo are ready to travel. Trace their vacation route to find out where they will be spending the summer. Name their destination in the space provided. List the places they will visit en route.

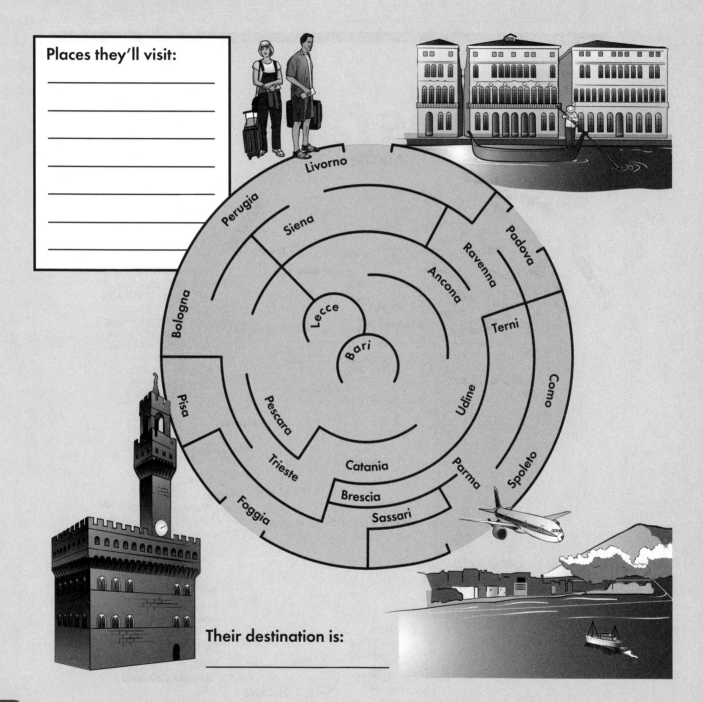

Places they'll visit:

_____
_____
_____
_____
_____
_____

Their destination is:
_____

K Tocca a te! Play travel agency! Pretend that you are going on a trip to Italy. Ask for recommendations of places to visit. Your friend will play the part of the travel agent and make several suggestions. You might also like to say hello, and later, say thank you in Italian!

trenitalia *informa*

la rete Eurostar Italia

Treni ad alta tecnologia, orari cadenzati, stazioni rinnovate, sistemi di vendita informatizzati, accoglienza a bordo ricca di servizi: tutto questo è Eurostar Italia. Un modo di viaggiare costituito da un insieme di servizi integrati, ad alto standard qualitativo, che accompagnano il cliente Trenitalia in ogni fase del suo viaggio. Protagonisti di Eurostar Italia sono le prestazioni all'avanguardia, le comodità, la convenienza ma soprattutto gli utenti del treno con le loro esigenze e aspettative.

Il servizio Eurostar Italia "viaggia" con gli ETR 500, 460, 480 e 450: il massimo del comfort integrato alla tecnologia

Look at the clipping and answer the following questions.

    1. What do you think *Treni* means?

          Train

    2. What city is the capital of Italy?

          Roma

    3. Is the capital located in the north, in the center, or in the south of Italy?

          Center

    4. Name the following cities with their Italian names:

        A. Milan Milano

        B. Venice Venezia

        C. Florence Firenza

        D. Naples Napoli

M   **Look at the map and answer the following questions:**

    1. Can you name the two big Italian islands?

    2. The Mediterranean Sea has four different names when it touches the coast of Italy. Can you name the following?

        A. The sea by Genova Mare Ligure

        B. The sea by Rome Mare Tirreno

        C. The sea between Reggio Calabria and Lecce Mare Ionio

        D. The sea between Trieste and Bari Mare Adriático

Proverbio

  " Tutte le strade portano a Roma.
  All roads lead to Rome. **"**

Symtalk

N Scrivi nello spazio la parola giusta in italiano. *(In the space, write the correct word in Italian.)*

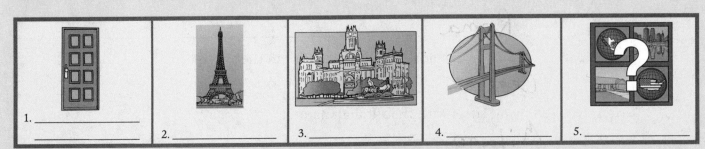

1. _____
_____

2. _____

3. _____

4. _____

5. _____

O Dì le frasi, poi scrivile in italiano. *(Say the sentences, then write them in Italian.)*

1. _____

2. _____

3. _____

4. _____

Fate le domande e rispondete. Poi, scrivete il dialogo. *(With a partner, ask the question or give the answer. Then, write the dialogue.)*

1.

_____

2.

_____

3.

_____

4.

_____

5.

_____

Il cruciverba

Orizzontale

2. largest seaport (Italian spelling)
4. statue sculpted by Michelangelo
5. mountain range (English spelling)
7. island (Italian spelling)
9. site of the Colosseum (Italian spelling)
10. national airline of Italy
12. river (include article)
13. city famous for ice cream (Italian spelling)

Verticale

1. site of Greek theater (Italian spelling)
3. site of the Grand Canal (Italian spelling)
6. geographical shape of Italy
8. Renaissance painter and architect of Florence's bell tower.
10. river
11. mountain range (Italian spelling)
14. river

Unit 5

La casa

House

Il vocabolario

SARA:	**Dove abiti?**	Where do you live?
PIETRO:	**Io abito in una casa a Roma.**	I live in a house in Rome.
ANNA:	**Dov'è il giardino?**	Where is the garden?
ALVARO:	**Il giardino è lì.**	The garden is over there.
GIUSEPPE:	**Dov'è il garage?**	Where's the garage?
FILIPPO:	**È dietro al giardino.**	It's behind the garden.
CLAUDIA:	**Quante camere ci sono nella tua casa?**	How many bedrooms are there in your house?
CASSANDRA:	**Ci sono quattro camere.**	There are four bedrooms.

In Italian, there are six words for **the**:

- *il* (in front of a masculine singular noun beginning with a **regular** consonant)
- *lo* (in front of a masculine singular noun beginning with a **z, ps, gn, y,** and **s** when followed by another consonant)
- *la* (in front of a feminine singular noun beginning with a consonant)
  lo and *la* contract to become *l'* before a singular noun beginning with a vowel to make pronunciation easier.
- *i* (in front of a masculine plural noun beginning with a **regular** consonant)
- *gli* (in front of a masculine plural noun beginning with a **z, ps, gn, y, s** plus a consonant **and** in front of masculine plural nouns beginning with vowels)
- *le* (in front of **all** feminine plural nouns, consonants, or vowels)

Vocabolario extra

la villa

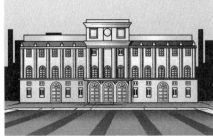

il palazzo

la casa

lo stabile/il palazzo/il condominio

l'appartamento

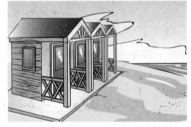

la cabina

la tenda

Appartamento is the equivalent for either condominium or apartment and is only a single unit—not the entire building.

Le attività

Scrivi la parola italiana per ogni stanza. *(Write the Italian word for each room.)*

1. _____la terrazza_____
2. _____il bagno_____
3. _____la cucina_____
4. _____la sala da pranzo_____

5. _____il salone_____
6. _____la camera_____
7. _____la terrazza_____
_____il cortile_____

B **Completa le frasi in italiano.** *(Complete the sentences in Italian with the appropriate house-related vocabulary.)*

1. Io cucino *(cook)* in _____.

2. Io dormo *(sleep)* nella mia _____.

3. Io mangio *(eat)* nella _____.

4. Io mi lavo *(take a bath)* nel _____.

5. Io gioco *(play)* nel _____.

6. Io mi riposo *(relax)* in _____ o in _____.

C Scegli la parola corretta per ogni stanza. *(Choose the correct translation for each room.)*

1. la sala da pranzo: bedroom   kitchen   (dining room)
2. la cucina: bathroom   (kitchen)   bedroom
3. la camera: (bedroom)   bathroom   living room
4. il bagno: dining room   kitchen   (bathroom)
5. il salone: (living room)   bathroom   dining room

D In which room would you find the following items? *In italiano, per favore.*

1. the dining table _____
2. the refrigerator _____
3. an alarm clock _____
4. a piano _____
5. the shower _____
6. the stove _____
7. a sofa _____
8. a tablecloth _____
9. the toilet _____
10. a dresser _____

E Identify each description with the appropriate Italian word.

1. place to sleep when camping _____
2. renter's residence in a building _____
3. homeowner's residence _____
4. millionaire's residence _____
5. place to park a car at home _____

F Riordina le parole. *(Unscramble the words.)*

1. ICNACU   Cucina
2. ESLANO _____
3. ADLAPZOSARNA _____
4. MECAAR _____
5. ETRAZRAZ _____

G **Leggi il paragrafo. Poi, scegli le parole corrette per completare ogni frase. (Read the paragraph. Then, choose the correct words to complete each sentence.)**

> La mia casa è *bella*. Abito *qui con* la mia famiglia. *Mi piace* la mia casa. Ci sono tre camere e un garage. Ci sono molti *fiori* in giardino e una *fontana* in terrazza.

casa

famiglia

bella	pretty	**mi piace**	I like	**mia**	my
quí	here	**fiori**	flowers		
con	with	**fontana**	fountain		

1. La mia famiglia abita in __.
   A. un giardino
   B. una camera
   C. una casa
   D. una terrazza

2. La casa è __.
   A. la mia famiglia
   B. un garage
   C. una terrazza
   D. bella

3. In giardino ci sono molti __.
   A. fiori
   B. famiglie
   C. fontane
   D. case

4. Ci sono __ camere nella casa.
   A. 8
   B. 3
   C. 6
   D. 5

H **Parliamo!** Point to a picture of a room in a house. Ask your speaking partner in Italian: "Is that a bedroom?" He/she should answer: "No, that's a kitchen." or "Yes, that's a bedroom." Take turns asking and answering about all the rooms in the house.

I Point to one of the types of homes shown in your book. As you do this, ask your classmate where an imaginary student lives. He/she should answer appropriately.

> **Modello:** A: *(points to an apartment)* Dove abita Ernesto?
> B: Ernesto abita in un appartamento.

J **Tocca a te!** Find out where people live. With your partner make a list of five famous people. Then ask your classmate in Italian: *Dove abita . . .?* adding the name of a famous person. Your classmate should answer by writing down the city or country in his/her notebook.

Lingua viva!

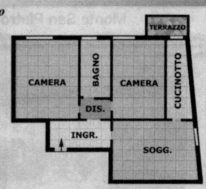

Look at the two floor plans on this clipping and answer the following questions:

1. How many bedrooms does the S. Lazzaro plan offer?

   _____

2. And how many bathrooms?

   _____

3. What is an *ingresso*?

   _____

4. You already know that a *cucina* is a kitchen, what do you think *cucinotto* means?

   _____

5. Both plans offer a *cantina*; what is a *cantina*?

   _____

   _____

L **Firenze is a well known Italian city. On this clipping are some offers for rental units called *affitti*. Can you find the following information?**

1. What is the address of this agency?

   _____

2. How much is the monthly rent for the unit called "Fiesole"?

   _____

3. In the unit called "Campo di Marte" there is an *ascensore*, what do you think it is?

   _____

4. In the unit called "Centro" with only 1100 euro you can live in an historical place, explain.

   _____

Proverbio

" **In casa sua ciascuno é re.**
Everyone is the king of his own castle. "

Symtalk

M Scrivi nello spazio la parola giusta in italiano. *(In the space, write the correct word in Italian.)*

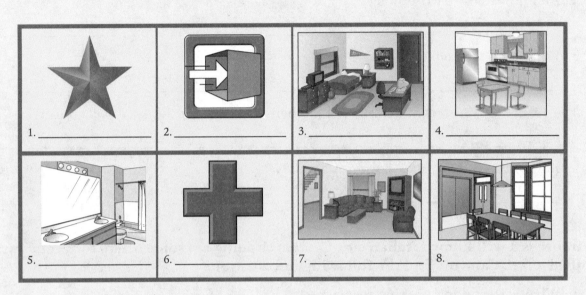

1. _____
2. _____
3. _____
4. _____
5. _____
6. _____
7. _____
8. _____

N Dì le frasi, poi scrivile in italiano. *(Say the sentences, then write them in Italian.)*

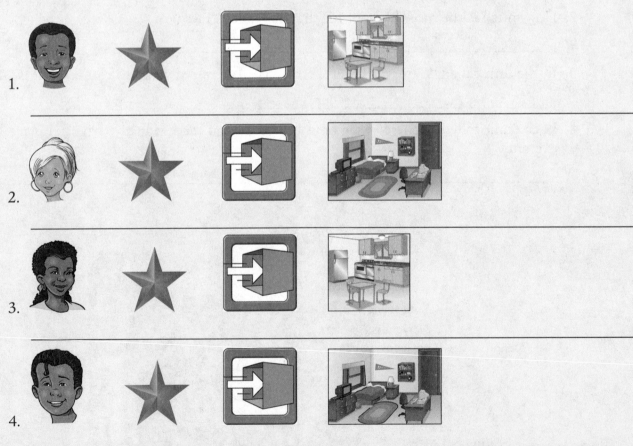

1. _____

2. _____

3. _____

4. _____

Fate le domande e rispondete. Poi, scrivete il dialogo. *(With a partner, ask the question or give the answer. Then, write the dialogue.)*

1.

   _____ | _____

   _____ | _____

2.

   _____ | _____

   _____ | _____

3.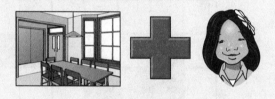

   _____ | _____

   _____ | _____

4.

   _____ | _____

   _____ | _____

5.

   _____ | _____

   _____ | _____

Il cruciverba

Orizzontale

1. place to bathe
6. behind, in back of (two words)
8. rented residence
10. place to dine (three words)
13. country home

Verticale

2. place to plant flowers
3. place to prepare food
4. _____ bedrooms are there? (how many)
5. place to relax or receive visitors
7. one word for bedroom
9. there are (two words)
11. _____ camere della casa
12. _____ abiti (tu)?

Unit 6

La famiglia

Family

Il vocabolario

i nonni
grandparents

la nonna
grandmother

il nonno
grandfather

il marito
husband

i genitori
parents

la moglie
wife

lo zio
uncle

la zia
aunt

il padre
father

la madre
mother

i figli
children

la sorella
sister

i fratelli
siblings

il fratello
brother

la nipote
niece

la cugina (female)
cousin

il nipote
nephew

il cugino (male)
cousin

il figlio
son

il nipote
grandson

la figlia
daughter

la nipote
granddaughter

The following are some conversations that might be overheard at a family reunion:

Chi è?
Who is this?

È mio fratello.
He's my brother.

Sono i tuoi genitori?
Are they your parents?

Sì, mia madre si chiama Cristina e mio padre si chiama Giuseppe.
Yes. My mother's name is Cristina and my father's name is Giuseppe.

Chi sono i bambini?
Who are the children?

Sono mia nipote e mio nipote.
They're my granddaughter and my grandson.

Suzanna, Nicola e Carlo sono fratelli, non è vero?
Susanna, Nicola, and Carlo are siblings, aren't they?

Sì, e sono anche i miei cugini.
Yes, and they are also my cousins.

Non dimenticare! riunione di famiglia gli invitati
Don't forget! Family Reunion Guests

- **Zia Margherita e suo marito**
  Aunt Margherita and her husband
- **Mia sorella e i suoi figli**
  my sister and her children
- **Zio Fabio e sua moglie**
  Uncle Fabio and his wife
- **Patrizia e il bambino**
  Patrizia and the baby

ELEONORA: **Dove sono i tuoi parenti?**
Where are your relatives?

ANDREA: **I miei nonni sono dentro e i miei zii e le mie zie sono in giardino.**
My grandparents are inside, and my uncles and aunts are in the garden.

GIORGIA: **Il tuo padrino e la tua madrina sono qui?**
Are your godfather and godmother here?

ROBERTO: **Sì, certo! La mia madrina sta parlando con le mie zie. Il mio padrino è in terrazza.**
Yes, of course! My godmother is speaking with my aunts. My godfather is on the terrace.

Vocabolario extra

il figlio
child (m)

il ragazzo
boy

la figlia
child (f)

l'uomo
man

la ragazza
girl

la donna
woman

il bambino/la bambina
baby (child)

il fratellastro
stepbrother

il patrigno
stepfather

il figliastro
stepson

la sorellastra
stepsister

la matrigna
stepmother

la figliastra
stepdaughter

Da notare: Use of the step-family member terms does not always have the best connotation. It is often better to explain the relationship.

Godparents play an important part in a child's life. Their main role is to offer encouragement and spiritual guidance as the child grows. It is customary for godparents to remember every birthday with a small gift. However, on special occasions—such as a first communion—it is anticipated that a more significant gift such as a golden bracelet or an expensive watch be given.

Le attività

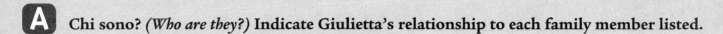

A Chi sono? *(Who are they?)* Indicate Giulietta's relationship to each family member listed.

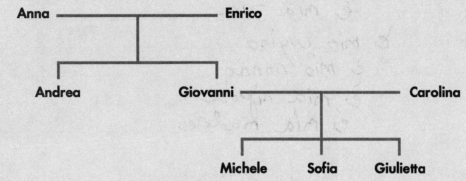

Giulietta è . . .

1. _____la sorella_____ di Michele.
2. _____la figlia_____ di Carolina.
3. _____la nipote_____ di Enrico.
4. _____la sorella_____ di Sofia.
5. _____la nipote_____ di Anna.
6. _____ di Andrea.
7. _____ di Giovanni.

B Fai lo stesso per Giovanni e Enrico. *(Do the same for Giovanni and Enrico.)*

Giovanni è il . . .

1. _____ di Michele, Sofia, e Giulietta.
2. _____ di Carolina.
3. _____ di Andrea.
4. _____figlio_____ di Anna e Enrico.

Enrico è il . . .

5. _____ di Michele, Sofia, e Giulietta.
6. _____ di Andrea e Giovanni.
7. _____ di Anna.

C   **Chi è?** *(Who is this?)* **Scrivi in italiano, per favore.**

> **Modello:** La figlia di mio padre e di mia madre è <u>mia sorella</u>.

1. La sorella di mia madre <u>è mia zia</u>.
2. Il figlio di mia zia <u>è mio cugino</u>.
3. Il padre di mia madre <u>è mio nonno</u>.
4. La figlia di mia sorella <u>è mia nipote</u>.
5. La madre di mia sorella <u>è mia madre</u>.

D   **Chi sono?** *(Who am I?)* **Scrivi in italiano, per favore.**

1. I am your father's son. I am your <u>fratello</u>.
2. I am your niece's mother. I am your <u>sorella</u>.
3. I am your brother's son. I am your <u>nipote</u>.
4. I am your mother's mother. I am your <u>~~nella~~ nonna</u>.

E **Scegli la risposta giusta.** *(Choose the correct answer.)*

1. Dove sono i genitori?
   A. next to the crib
   B. in the crib
   C. in the foreground

2. Dov'è il bambino?
   A. next to the crib
   B. in the crib
   C. in the foreground

3. Dove sono i nonni?
   A. next to the crib
   B. in the crib
   C. in the foreground

F In inglese. *(What do these questions mean in English?)*

1. Chi è?

   _____

2. Chi sono?

   _____

3. Chi è la donna?

   _____

4. Chi parla con la zia Isabella?

   _____

G Completa in italiano. *(Complete each question in Italian.)* **Use the cues in parentheses.**

1. Chi è il ragazzo? *(son)*

   È mio _figlio_____.

2. Chi è la ragazza? *(cousin)*

   È mia _cugina_____.

3. Chi è l'uomo? *(uncle)*

   È mio _zio_____.

H Prova a tradurre il brano in inglese. *(Read the passage and then write it in English.)* **Just guess at the words you may not know! See how much you can figure out!**

> La mia famiglia non *è* grande. Mio padre ha trentasette anni. Mia madre ha trentotto anni. Mia sorella si chiama Raffaella e ha nove anni. Mio fratello si chiama Sandro e ha sei anni. Mi chiamo Chiara ed ho tredici anni. La mia famiglia abita a Roma. *Abbiamo* una casa. I miei nonni abitano a Firenze. *Hanno* un appartamento.

(Lui/Lei) è he/she is	**(Noi) abbiamo** we have	**(Loro) hanno** they have

_____

_____

_____

_____

_____

_____

I Parliamo! Ask your speaking partner about five members of his/her family. Ask about the name and age of each person. Your partner should answer each question. Then, he/she will ask you about your family and you will answer.

> Modello: A: Hai una sorella? *(Do you have a sister?)*
> B: Sì, ho una sorella.
> A: Come si chiama? *(What is her name?)*
> B: Si chiama Sara.
> A: Quanti anni ha? *(How old is she?)*
> B: Ha nove anni.

J Tocca a te! Find some family photographs and exchange them with a friend. Holding up your friend's photo first, ask him/her who is in the picture. He/she will identify each person with the correct relationship. Then, reverse roles.

> Modello: A: Chi è? *(Who is this?)*
> B: È mia nonna. *(That's my grandmother.)*

Proverbio

" Quale padre, tale figlio.
Like father, like son. "

Bello essere famiglia.

SOS Genitori

GENTE

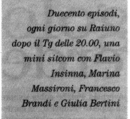

Duecento episodi, ogni giorno su Raiuno dopo il Tg delle 20.00, una mini sitcom con Flavio Insinna, Marina Massironi, Francesco Brandi e Giulia Bertini

"Cotti e mangiati"

speciale TV

...Una famiglia in cucina...

Duecento episodi, in onda su Raiuno ogni giorno dopo il Telegiornale delle 20.00: con *Cotti e mangiati* la Rai fa il primo tentativo di mini-sitcom. L'ambiente è unico, la cucina della famiglia Mancini, protagonista della serie, e le riprese vengono effettuate a camera fissa. Ogni puntata ha una durata di circa 25 minuti ed è divisa in quattro scene di sei minuti l'una.
I protagonisti sono quattro: Franco, il padre, Silvia, la madre, e i

figli Marco e Alessia. Franco, interpretato da Flavio Insinna (noto al pubblico televisivo per il ruolo del capitano Anceschi nella serie Don Matteo), è titolare di un autonoleggio. Sua moglie Silvia (Marina Massironi) è una professoressa di Lettere, cronicamente precaria. I figli Marco (Francesco Brandi), ventiduenne, e Alessia (Giulia Bertini), sedicenne, sono studenti.
A dare lo spunto alla serie è la vita quotidiana di questa famiglia di stampo piccolo borghese, alle prese con i piccoli e grandi problemi della realtà d'oggi. Le riprese di *Cotti e mangiati* sono iniziate lo scorso mese di aprile e si concluderanno a settembre, con il duecentesimo episodio. Naturalmente se gli indici di ascol-

to dimostreranno il gradimento del pubblico si potrà andare avanti, girando una seconda serie.
Per Flavio Insinna, dopo *Don Matteo*, un'altra occasione per sfruttare la sua vena di attore brillante. Le maggiori soddisfazioni, però, le ha avute come interprete drammatico, prima come protagonista di una fiction dedicata alla figura di Don Bosco e poi, più di recente, in *La buona battaglia*, indossando la tonaca di don Pietro Pappagallo, il sacerdote che è stato tr[...]
Fosse Ardeati[...]
to anche il film[...]
sellini *Roma c[...]
sinna dice di n[...]
lizzare", di sen[...]
tato per il gen[...]
comico, senza [...]

www.[...].it

Grazie di tutto nonno Ari e nonna Anna vi amo . . . Nina!

Un mondo di auguri di buon compleanno alla nostra meravigliosa Alessia per i suoi fantastici tre anni, che compi il 21 luglio. Con tanto amore nonna Sele e nonno Dante.

Caro papà, ti vogliamo tanto bene, Klara e Josef.

Volevo
dirti che...

K Find the clipping about a TV show that runs every day for 25 minutes and is called "Cotti e Mangiati." The show is about a typical middle class Italian family. With the help of this clipping, can you answer the following questions?

1. How many members are in this family?

   _____

2. The episodes are filmed in a specific area of the house, which one?

   _____

3. What is the name of the father of the family?

   _____

4. What is the name of the mother?

   _____

5. How old is Marco, the son?

   _____

6. How many total episodes will be run?

   _____

L Find the three personal ads from a local newspaper. Can you find the following information?

1. Klara and Joseph are writing to say "I love you" to whom?

   _____

2. Nina is rather young, but she is already thanking two very important people in her life. Can you tell who they are?

   _____

3. Alessia is celebrating a birthday; how old is she?

   _____

4. When is Alessia's birthday?

   _____

5. Who is writing to wish Alessia a happy birthday?

   _____

Symtalk

M Scrivi nello spazio la parola giusta in italiano. *(In the space, write the correct word in Italian.)*

1. _____ 2. _____ 3. _____ 4. _____ 5. _____ 6. _____

N Dì le frasi, poi scrivile in italiano. *(Say the sentences, then write them in Italian.)*

1. _____

2. _____

3. _____

4. _____

O

Fate le domande e rispondete. Poi, scrivete il dialogo. *(With a partner, ask the question or give the answer. Then, write the dialogue.)*

1. _____

2. _____

3. _____

4. _____

5. _____

Il cruciverba

Orizzontale

1. Il signor Rossi è un ____.
7. Una ____ è una giovane donna.
8. Una madre, un padre, e i figli sono una ____.
10. Gli zii, le zie, i cugini e i nonni sono i ____.
12. Mio ____ è il padre di mio padre.
14. Mio ____ è il figlio di mia madre e di mio padre.

Verticale

2. Mia ____ è la moglie di mio padre.
3. Un ____ è un giovane uomo.
4. Mia sorella è la ____ di mio padre e di mia madre.
5. La signora Bernardini è una ____.
6. Mia ____ è la figlia dei miei zii.
9. Mio ____ è il figlio di mia sorella.
10. Mio ____ è il marito di mia madre.
11. Mia ____ è la madre di mia madre.
13. Mio ____ è il fratello di mio padre.

Unit 7

Gli animali

Animals

Il vocabolario

una mucca
cow

un asino/un'asina
donkey

un uccello
bird

un'anatra
duck

un maiale/
una scrofa
pig

un gallo
rooster

una gallina
hen

un gatto/una gatta
cat

un cavallo/una cavalla
horse

un cane/una cagna
dog

MARIA: **Arturo, vieni! Do da mangiare agli animali adesso. Do una mela a Maurizio.**
Arturo, come on! I'm feeding the animals now. I'm giving Maurizio an apple.

ARTURO: **Bello! Posso aiutarti.**
Great! I can help you.

MARIA: **Certo che puoi, Arturo! Puoi tenere il secchio.**
Of course you can, Arturo! You can hold the bucket.

ARTURO: **Come si chiama il gatto (la gatta)?**
What's the cat's name?

MARIA: **È Alba.**
That's Alba.

ARTURO: **Ci sono anche delle galline?**
Are there hens, too?

MARIA: **Sì, sono dietro alla stalla. Puoi raccogliere le uova.**
Yes, they're behind the barn. You can gather the eggs.

in campagna
in the country

nell'aria
in the air

nel fienile
in the barn

un pappagallo
a parrot

nel campo
in the field

una capra
a goat

un animale
an animal

nello stagno
in the pond

nella stalla
in the stable

un coniglio
a rabbit

grande
big

piccolo
little

le uova
the eggs

ROBERTO:	**Che cosa fai?**
	What are you doing?
BEPPE:	**Raccolgo le uova.**
	I'm gathering the eggs.

ANTONIO:	**Che cosa fai?**
	What are you doing?
CHIARA:	**Accarezzo il mio coniglio.**
	I'm petting my rabbit.

Sounds that animals make:

La mucca "fa" muuu (moo).

Il cavallo "fa" hiii (neigh).

Il gatto "fa" miao (meow).

Il cane "fa" bau bau (woof).

Il maiale "fa" sgrunt/oinc (oink).

L'anatra "fa" qua qua, qua, qua (quack).

Il gallo "fa" chicchirichì (cocka-doodle-doo).

Le attività

 Come si chiama l'animale? *(Identify each animal in Italian.)*

1. È _____.

2. È _____.

3. È _____.

4. È _____.

5.   È _____.

B **Quale animale si trova di solito in questi posti?** *(Which animal can usually be found at each location?)* **Per favore scrivi la risposta in italiano.**

1. nel campo

_____

2. nella stalla

_____

3. nello stagno

_____

4. nell'aria

_____

5. nel fienile

_____

C **Dove? Chi? Che cosa? Quale? Scegli la risposta giusta.** *(Where? Who? What? Which? Choose the correct answer.)*

1. Dove sono Maria e Arturo?
   A. nello stagno
   B. nel campo
   C. in campagna

2. Dov'è il cavallo?
   A. nell'aria
   B. nella stalla
   C. nello stagno

3. Chi ha *(has)* una mela per *(for)* Maurizio?
   A. Maria
   B. Arturo
   C. il cavallo

4. Chi vuole *(wants)* aiutare?
   A. Maria
   B. Arturo
   C. Alba

5. Che cosa ha Maria? *(What does Maria have?)*
   A. una mucca
   B. una capra
   C. un secchio

6. Quale *(which)* animale è piccolo?
   A. l'uccello
   B. il maiale
   C. il cavallo

D **Completa le frasi correttamente.** *(Complete the sentences correctly.)*

1. _____ La gatta si chiama . . .   A. Maurizio

2. _____ L'asino è . . .   B. piccolo

3. _____ La mucca è al . . .   C. grande

4. _____ La mela è per . . .   D. Alba

5. _____ Il gallo è . . .   E. campo

E **Riordina dal più piccolo al più grande.** *(Rearrange this group of animals. Start with the smallest in size and end with the biggest.)*

la mucca   il coniglio   la capra   l'uccello

1. _____

2. _____

3. _____

4. _____

F **Com'è l'animale?** *(What is each animal like?)* **Indicate the size of each animal by choosing either little *(piccolo)* or big *(grande)*. Write out the full sentence in Italian.**

> **Modello:** Com'è un cavallo?
> Un cavallo è grande.

1. Com'è un asino?

   _____

2. Com'è un gatto?

   _____

3. Com'è una capra?

   _____

4. Com'è un maiale?

   _____

5. Com'è un gallo?

   _____

G What goes together? Match the Italian with the English. Focus on the familiar words and guess the others.

1. _____ Sono in campagna.
2. _____ Vedo gli animali.
3. _____ Posso aiutarti.
4. _____ Posso tenere il secchio.
5. _____ Do da mangiare al gatto.
6. _____ Posso raccogliere le uova.

A. I see the animals.
B. I want to help you.
C. I can gather the eggs.
D. I'm feeding the cat.
E. I can hold the pail.
F. I am in the country.

H **Parliamo!** Select four animals from this unit. Ask your speaking partner where each one is. He/she should answer correctly. Then, your partner asks you where four other animals are. You reply this time.

> **Modello:** **A:** Dov'è l'anatra?
> **B:** È nello stagno.

I **Tocca a te!** Find out whether your classmate knows the names of the animals. Offer a clue for each animal, such as sounds or actions: It oinks, it neighs, it meows, it barks, it moos, it warbles, it climbs, it swims, it gives eggs, it carries loads, or it twitches its whiskers. Make sure your classmate says *the* before each name. Next, your partner will give you a clue by naming a place, such as a field, pond, stable, air, or barn. You will say in Italian the name of the animal associated with each place.

Proverbio

" **Can che abbaia non morde.**
One's bark is worse than one's bite. "

Bau bau!

Lingua viva!

Stili di vita del gatto

Scopri caratteristiche, abitudini e differenze.

Vita **in casa**

Accesso **all'esterno**

ROYAL CANIN
FELINE HEALTH NUTRITION

DVD

La Battaglia delle Mucche

"La Battaglia delle Regine" è un evento del folklore valdostano che aiuta a preservare l'attaccamento alla terra e alle tradizioni, oltre che a selezionare i migliori esemplari da riproduzione.

Quasi 200 Regine dal carattere più aggressivo e battagliero si affrontano nella fase finale ad Aosta **il 22 ottobre**.

La vincitrice di ogni categoria riceve un bel campanaccio, trattenuto da un collare in cuoio, finemente e riccamente lavorato, oltre a un serto con pennacchio colorato e un nastro rosso, avvolgente lo stomaco.

J **Look at the cat clipping and answer the following questions.**

1. What do you think *"stili di vita"* means?

   _____

2. This ad talks about two different kind of lifestyles for cats; what are they?

   _____

3. What do you think the word *scopri* means?

   _____

4. This DVD teaches us about the *caratteristiche, abitudini,* and *differenze* in cats. Can you guess the English meanings of these three words?

   _____

K **The *"Battaglia delle mucche"* is a western alpine Italian tradition. Look at the clipping and answer the following questions:**

1. What does *mucche* mean?

   _____

2. What do you think *"La Battaglia Delle Mucche"* means?

   _____

L **The cows fight to become the champion of the queens. Each herd produces a queen that participates in the final tournament. The two fighting cows don't hurt each other; when one cow realizes that the other one is stronger, she just backs down. Look at the clipping and find the answers to the following questions:**

1. The word *regina* means queen. How many queens participate in the final tournament?

   _____

2. What is the date of the final tournament?

   _____

3. The word *nastro* means ribbon. See if you can find what color ribbon will decorate the grand champion.

Symtalk

M   Scrivi nello spazio la parola giusta in italiano. *(In the space, write the correct word in Italian.)*

1. _____
2. _____
3. _____
4. _____
5. _____
6. _____

N   Fai le domande e rispondi in italiano. *(Ask and answer the questions in Italian.)*

1. _____   _____

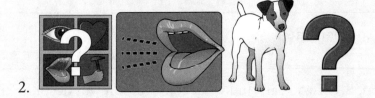

2. _____   _____

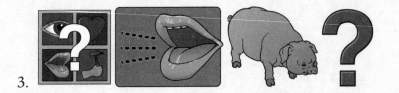

3. _____   _____

O Fate le domande e rispondete. Scrivete il dialogo. *(Work with a partner. After one of you asks the question, the other responds that no, the person likes a different kind of animal. Please write the dialogue in Italian.)*

1. _____

2. _____

3. _____

4. _____

5. _____

Il cruciverba

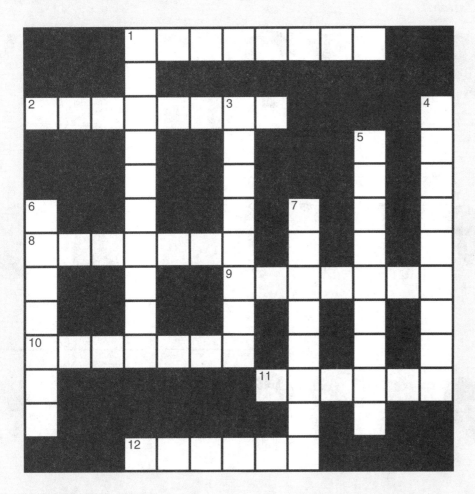

Orizzontale

1. small body of water
2. flies
8. swims and dives for food
9. gives us milk
10. has kittens
11. animal that helps us carry things
12. barks

Verticale

1. country
3. resting place for an animal
4. trots and gallops
5. bucket
6. wakes up people in the morning
7. oinks

Unit 8

I mestieri

Occupations

Il vocabolario

l'artista
artist

**l'uomo d'affari
la donna d'affari**
businessman, businesswoman

l'elettricista
electrician

il falegname
carpenter

**il cuoco/
la cuoca/lo chef**
cook, chef

l'infermiere/a
nurse

il meccanico
mechanic

**il medico
il dottore**
physician

il/la musicista
musician

**l'insegnante
il professore/
la professoressa**
teacher

**l'agricoltore
l'agricoltrice**
farmer

**il postino
la postina**
letter carrier

l'idraulico
plumber

**il programmatore
la programmatrice**
computer programmer

Dove lavori?
Where do you work?

Lavoro in campagna. Sono agricoltrice.
I work in the country. I am a farmer.

Ti piace lavorare?
Do you like to work?

Sì, mi piace lavorare.
Yes, I like to work.

Qual'è la tua professione? Qual'è il tuo mestiere? Che lavoro fai?
What is your profession?

Sono attore./Faccio l'attore.
I am an actor.

Che cosa fai (come lavoro)? Quale lavoro fai?
What do you do (for a living)?

Sono attrice. Lavoro nel teatro.
I am an actress. I work at the theater.

Le attività

A **Metti il numero accanto al mestiere.** *(Number in order the professions or trades as your teacher says each one.)*

_____ il medico

_____ il meccanico

_____ il postino

_____ lo chef

_____ l'uomo d'affari

_____ l'elettricista

_____ l'agricoltore

_____ il programmatore

_____ l'insegnante

_____ il musicista

B **Chi lavora qui?** *(Who works here?)*

1. restaurant _____

2. wood shop _____

3. post office _____

4. school _____

5. auto service station _____

6. dairy barn _____

7. stage _____

8. hospital _____

9. studio _____

10. office _____

C **Trova la parola giusta.** *(Unscramble the words.)*

1. ODIAULCIR _____

2. OTETAR _____

3. ITARATS _____

4. SOPNITO _____

5. ROMGRAMTORAEP _____

D **Completa le frasi.** *Use the clues in parentheses.*

1. Qual'è il tuo _____? *(occupation)*

2. _____ attrice. *(I am)*

3. _____ nel teatro. *(I work)*

4. Dove _____, Paolo? *(do you work)*

5. Io lavoro _____ cucina. *(in)*

6. Che cosa _____? *(do you do)*

7. Io sono _____. *(cook)*

8. _____ lavorare. *(I like)*

E **Come si dice in inglese?** *(How do you say this in English?)* **Look first, then take a good guess. Write out each sentence in English.**

1. Mia madre è interprete.

   _____

2. Lei parla tedesco e portoghese.

   _____

3. Mio padre è musicista.

   _____

4. Lui suona la chitarra.

   _____

5. Mia cugina è programmatrice.

   _____

6. Lei lavora con un computer.

   _____

7. Mio cugino è cuoco.

   _____

8. Lui prepara il cibo.

   _____

I mestieri

F

Indovina chi ? *(Guess who? Some may be male, and others female.)* **In italiano, per favore.**

1. *La* _____ creates software.

2. *Il* _____ is in charge of healing sick people.

3. *L'* _____ checks for faulty wiring.

4. *Il* _____ installs wooden beams.

5. *L'* _____ paints portraits.

6. *Il* _____ cooks food.

7. *La* _____ manages a company.

8. *L'* _____ plants and harvests.

9. *Il* _____ delivers mail.

10. *Il* _____ plays in a symphony orchestra.

G

Scrivi il nome italiano della professione che corrisponde ad ogni immagine. *(In Italian, write the name of the profession that corresponds to each picture.)*

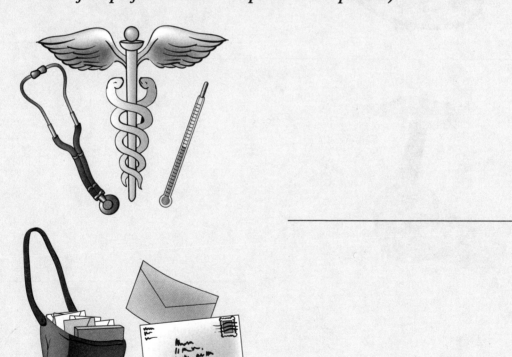

1. _____

2. _____

3. _____

4. _____

5. _____

H **Parliamo!** Guess a person's occupation. Give your speaking partner a cue. For example, you say "hospital" and your partner will say, *il medico*. Then he/she gives you a cue, such as "paintbrush" and you will say, *l'artista*. Ask about five occupations each and take turns.

I **Tocca a te!** Help create a classroom bulletin-board display about occupations. Cut out pictures from magazines showing people in all the occupations listed in this unit. Label each one in Italian, for example, *Lei è un'artista* or *Lui è uomo d'affari*. Label the entire display as *Mestieri*.

Lingua viva!

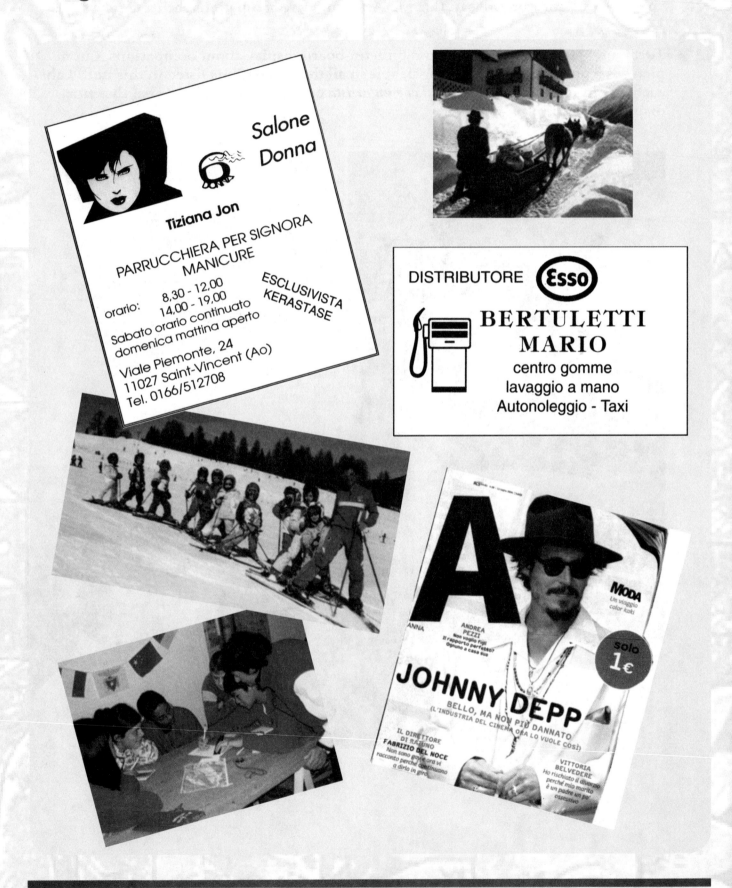

Salone Donna

Tiziana Jon

PARRUCCHIERA PER SIGNORA
MANICURE

orario: 8.30 - 12.00
14.00 - 19.00

Sabato orario continuato
domenica mattina aperto

ESCLUSIVISTA
KERASTASE

Viale Piemonte, 24
11027 Saint-Vincent (Ao)
Tel. 0166/512708

DISTRIBUTORE **Esso**

BERTULETTI MARIO

centro gomme
lavaggio a mano
Autonoleggio - Taxi

A

MODA
Un viaggio
color kaki

solo
1€

ANNA   ANDREA PEZZI
Non voglio figli
Il rapporto perfetto?
Ognuno a casa sua

JOHNNY DEPP
BELLO, MA NON PIÙ DANNATO
(L'INDUSTRIA DEL CINEMA ORA LO VUOLE COSÌ)

IL DIRETTORE
DI RAIUNO
FABRIZIO DEL NOCE
Non sono gay ora vi
racconto perché continuano
a dirlo in giro

VITTORIA
BELVEDERE
Ho rischiato il divorzio
perché mio marito
è un padre un po'
ossessivo

J **Look at the hair stylist ad and answer the following questions:**

1. Can you find the Italian word for "hair stylist"?

   _____

2. In this ad, there are two words that mean "woman," can you find them?

   _____

3. How long is the break for lunch?

   _____

4. *Orario continuato* means non-stop; which day of the week is this store open non-stop?

   _____

5. Is this store open on Sunday?

   _____

K **Look at the ESSO gas station ad and answer the following questions.**

1. Which Italian word is used for "gas station" in this ad?

   _____

2. The following are other services offered at this gas station. Can you guess what they are in English?

   A. *Centro Gomme* _____

   B. *Lavaggio a mano* _____

   C. *Autonoleggio* _____

Proverbio

" **Nessuno nasce maestro.**
Practice makes perfect. "

Symtalk

Scrivi nello spazio la parola giusta in italiano. *(In the space, write the correct word in Italian.)*

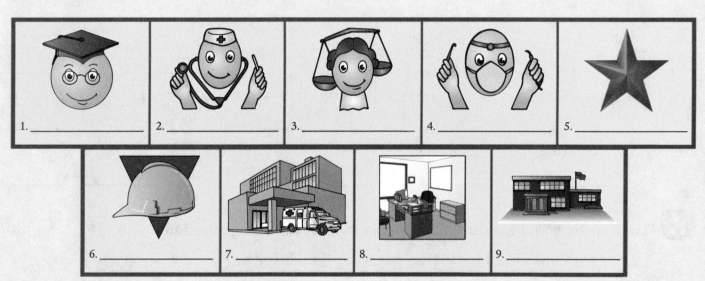

1. _____

2. _____

3. _____

4. _____

5. _____

6. _____

7. _____

8. _____

9. _____

M **Dí le frasi, poi scrivile in italiano.** *(Say the sentences, then write them in Italian.)*

1. _____

2. _____

3. _____

4.

Fate le domande e rispondete. Poi, scrivete il dialogo. *(With a partner, ask the question or give the answer. Then, write the dialogue.)*

1.

_____

2.

_____

3.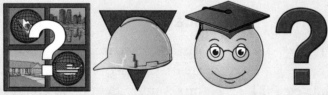

_____

4.

_____

Il cruciverba

For this crossword puzzle, use a form of the definite article *(the)* before each word.

Orizzontale

1. paints, draws, or sculpts *(m., f.)*
4. repairs broken engines *(m.)*
7. installs sinks and fixes leaking faucets *(m.)*
8. plays in a band or orchestra *(m.)*
9. builds things with wood *(m.)*

Verticale

1. installs electrical wiring in a house *(m., f.)*
2. treats sick people *(m.)*
3. mixes ingredients and creates meals *(f.)*
5. performs on stage *(f.)*
6. delivers letters, magazines, and postcards *(m.)*

Unit 9

Il cibo

Food

Vocabolario

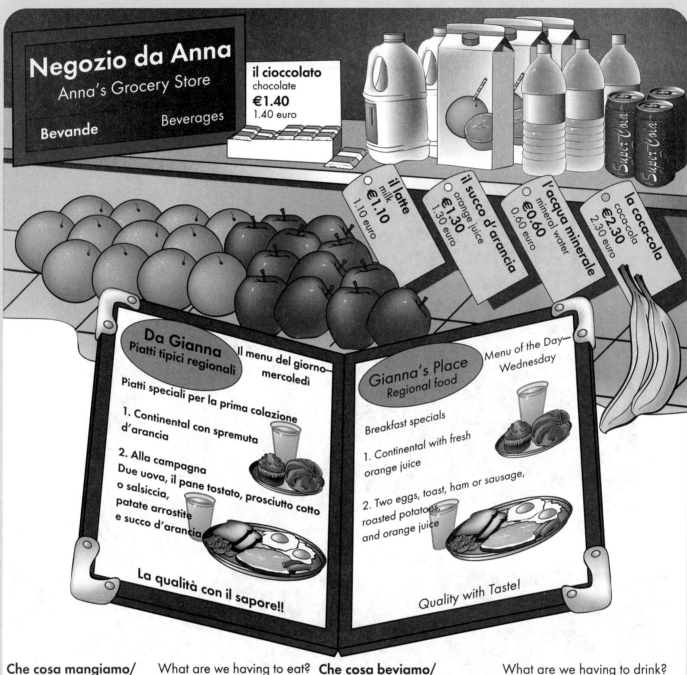

Negozio da Anna
Anna's Grocery Store

Bevande   Beverages

il cioccolato
chocolate
€1.40
1.40 euro

il latte
milk
€1.10
1.10 euro

il succo d'arancia
orange juice
€1.30
1.30 euro

l'acqua minerale
mineral water
€0.60
0.60 euro

la coca-cola
coca-cola
€2.30
2.30 euro

Da Gianna
Piatti tipici regionali

Il menu del giorno—
mercoledì

Piatti speciali per la prima colazione

1. Continental con spremuta d'arancia

2. Alla campagna
Due uova, il pane tostato, prosciutto cotto o salsiccia, patate arrostite e succo d'arancia

La qualità con il sapore!!

Gianna's Place
Regional food

Menu of the Day—
Wednesday

Breakfast specials

1. Continental with fresh orange juice

2. Two eggs, toast, ham or sausage, roasted potatoes and orange juice

Quality with Taste!

Che cosa mangiamo/ prendiamo?	What are we having to eat?	**Che cosa beviamo/ prendiamo?**	What are we having to drink?
Mangiamo un'insalata./ Prendiamo un'insalata.	We're having salad.	**Beviamo un bicchiere di latte./ Prendiamo un bicchiere di latte.**	We're having a glass of milk.
Hai fame?	Are you hungry?	**Hai sete, Roberto?**	Are you thirsty, Roberto?
Sì, ho fame.	Yes. I'm hungry.	**No, non ho sete.**	No, I'm not thirsty.
Che cosa mangi?	What are you eating?	**Che cosa bevi, Susanna?**	What are you drinking, Suzanna?
Mangio un panino.	I'm eating a sandwich.	**Bevo un bicchiere di latte.**	I'm drinking a glass of milk.

La frutta

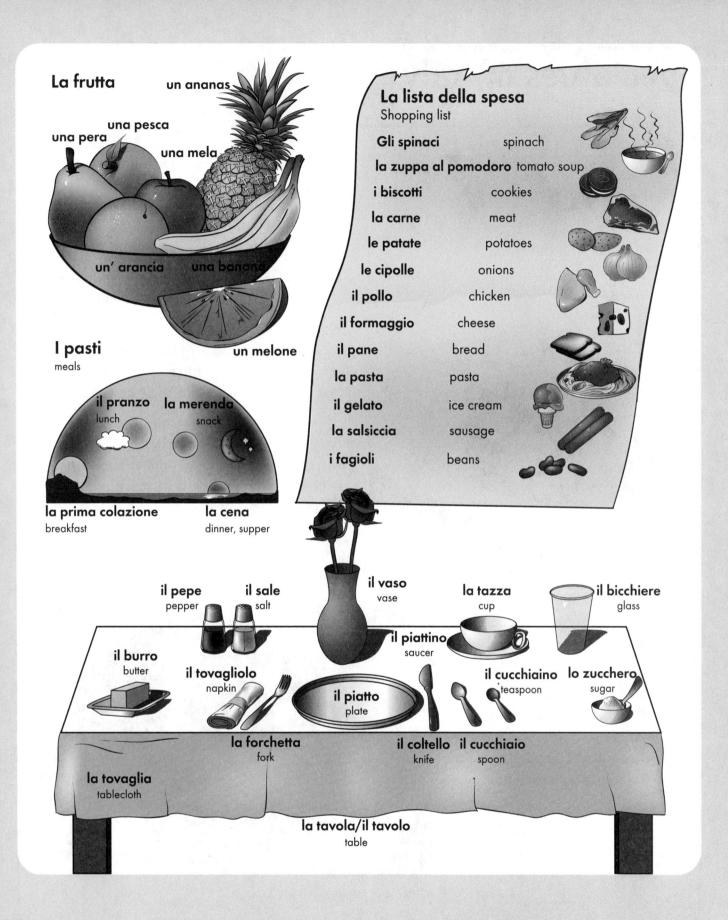

un ananas

una pesca

una pera

una mela

un' arancia   una banana

un melone

I pasti
meals

il pranzo   la merenda
lunch   snack

la prima colazione   la cena
breakfast   dinner, supper

La lista della spesa
Shopping list

Gli spinaci	spinach
la zuppa al pomodoro	tomato soup
i biscotti	cookies
la carne	meat
le patate	potatoes
le cipolle	onions
il pollo	chicken
il formaggio	cheese
il pane	bread
la pasta	pasta
il gelato	ice cream
la salsiccia	sausage
i fagioli	beans

il pepe   il sale   il vaso   la tazza   il bicchiere
pepper   salt   vase   cup   glass

                                          il piattino
                                          saucer

il burro   il cucchiaino   lo zucchero
butter   il tovagliolo   teaspoon   sugar
            napkin   il piatto
                            plate

            la forchetta   il coltello   il cucchiaio
            fork   knife   spoon

la tovaglia
tablecloth

la tavola/il tavolo
table

Specialties of Italy

Zuppa di pesce with shrimp

Frittata—omelet commonly prepared with chopped onion and chopped sweet peppers. Shellfish, meat, or vegetables also may be added.

Fonduta Piemontese—a creamy sauce made of melted fontina cheese, eggs, milk, and whittle truffles. It is eaten with polenta.

Zuppa di pesce—fish soup containing pieces of fish flavored with onion, garlic, and chopped parsley. When offered as a main dish, it may be served with warm bread and cheese.

Risotto Portofino—casserole of rice, chicken, and shrimp, flavored with onion, garlic, black pepper, and rosemary. This dish takes its name from the city in which it is most popular, Portofino.

Pollo alla cacciatora—chicken hunter-style, chicken cooked and served in a flavorful tomato sauce seasoned with garlic, onion, oregano, white wine, and pepper. This dish is generally served with mashed potatoes.

Vitello alla parmigiana—veal cutlet breaded, fried, then baked in a zesty tomato sauce and topped with mozzarella cheese. It is a popular specialty from the region of Parma.

Saltimbocca—strip of boned veal wrapped in ham, fried in butter, and seasoned to taste.

Vitello alla parmigiana with spaghetti

Osso buco—veal shanks prepared with carrots, onion, and celery and flavored with garlic, thyme, bay leaf, and black pepper. Rice often accompanies this dish.

Osso buco with risotto

Zabaglione

Panforte—sugar cake containing almonds, honey, and candied fruit, generally melon, lemon, or orange.

Zabaglione—custard dessert composed chiefly of egg yolks, sugar, and Marsala wine. This dessert is as creamy and rich as its name implies.

- *Buon appetito!* is a wish on the part of a friend or host for all guests to enjoy the meal and eat heartily.
- The name of a certain food can vary even within Italy. For example, *pizza bianca* is a flat white salty bread (essentially plain cooked pizza dough) in Rome, while in Florence it is called *schiacciata*. This form of bread can be called focaccia also. A breaded fried ball of rice with mozzarella (and a variety of other ingredients chosen by the chef) can be called *un suppli* or *un arancino* (it looks like an orange).
- *A tavola!* is an expression that invites the family and guests to gather at the table and begin the meal.

Le attività

 A Scrivi il nome italiano per ogni oggetto. *(Write the Italian name of each object.)*

1. _____

2. _____

3. _____

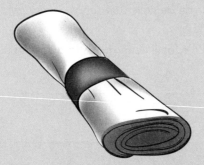

4. _____

5. _____

6. _____

7. _____

8. _____

B Completa ogni frase in inglese. *(Complete each sentence in English.)*

1. A custard dessert popular in Italy is _____.

2. The three main ingredients found in *Risotto Portofino* are _____,
   _____, and _____.

3. A popular dish from the region of Parma is _____.

4. A _____ is an omelet served for lunch and/or dinner.

5. The principal ingredient in *Zuppa di pesce* is _____.

C Che cosa appartiene ad ogni categoria? *(Using your food vocabulary and the list of specialties, write three food items for each of the following categories.)*

1. **meat**

   A. _____

   B. _____

   C. _____

2. **vegetables**

   A. _____

   B. _____

   C. _____

3. **dairy products**

   A. _____

   B. _____

   C. _____

4. **beverages**

   A. _____

   B. _____

   C. _____

5. **fruits**

   A. _____

   B. _____

   C. _____

6. **desserts**

   A. _____

   B. _____

   C. _____

D Imagine you are opening a restaurant in Italy. From your food and specialty lists, prepare a menu for lunch and dinner. At least three dishes or items for each meal should be offered.

E Prepare a poster from magazine pictures. Show a balanced breakfast and a balanced dinner. Label each food item with its Italian name.

F Prepare fifteen different flash cards with a picture of a food item on one side and its Italian name on the other. Present your flash cards to the class.

G Un gioco. Working in small groups, list in Italian twenty foods or beverages. Then, scramble each word. The student who correctly unscrambles the most words first will be the winner.

H Parliamo! Your classmate is in charge of the menu today. In Italian, tell her (him) that you are hungry. You want to know what there is to eat today. She will tell you five foods. Next, she will tell you that she is thirsty and ask you what there is to drink. Answer accordingly and name five beverages.

I Tocca a te! Imagine that you work at a very nice restaurant in Portofino. A customer asks you about a regional specialty, such as *Risotto Portofino*. Explain what this specialty is and how it is made.

Proverbio

" Non tutte le ciambelle riescono con il buco.
Not everything you do can be perfect. "

Lingua viva!

penne rigate 70

spaghetti 4

Pasta di semola coop
1 kg, formati vari

€ 0,84

€ **0,50**

Intermezzo

Caffè Intermezzo "Segafredo"
macinato
4x250 g

€ 5,90

€ **3,54**

Coppa Del Nonno MOTTA
Caffè/Cappuccino
g 280/g 300

15 PUNTI

6 Panini
SAN CARLO
g 360

10 PUNTI

Müesli Vitalis CAMEO
gusti assortiti
g 375

VITALIS
VITALIS
MÜESLI
CROCCANTE

10 PUNTI

Aromito Piccante
ITALPEPE
Busta/Barattolo
g 100/g 130

20 PUNTI

Numero Verde
☏ **800-456654**
Numero Verde
da Lunedì a Sabato
dalle ore 9.00
alle ore 20.00

díperdí

OGNI GIORNO MI SORRIDE.

servizio.clienti@diperdi.it

www.diperdi.it

Olio Extra Vergine
di Oliva Fraticello
"Coricelli"
750 ml

€ 5,69

€ **3,41**

J **Look at the clippings and answer the following questions.**

1. The ice cream *Coppa del Nonno* is offered in many different flavors. Can you tell which two are represented in this clipping?

   _____

2. Find the Italian word for sandwiches.

   _____

3. In the cereal ad for Vitalis Cameo, can you guess what *gusti assortiti* means?

   _____

4. You can get more information about these products by calling the 800 number on the ad. When can you call? Please write the days and time that you can call.

   _____

5. The *Aromito Piccante* is a spice that is sold in two different types of packaging. What do you think *Busta* and *Barattolo* mean?

   _____

K **Look at the clippings and answer the following questions.**

1. How big is the bottle of extra virgin olive oil?

   _____

2. How much is the price for one liter of olive oil?

   _____

3. What do you think the word *macinato* means?

   _____

4. For 1 euro, how much pasta can you buy?

   _____

5. How many packets of coffee can you buy with 3.54 euros?

   _____

6. Look at the prices in euros. Would they be written the same way if they were in dollars? If not, what is the difference?

   _____

Symtalk

L Scrivi nello spazio la parola giusta in italiano. *(In the space, write the correct word in Italian.)*

1. _____ 2. _____ 3. _____ 4. _____ 5. _____ 6. _____

M Dì le frasi, poi scrivile in italiano. *(Say the sentences, then write them in Italian.)*

1. _____

2. _____

3. _____

4. _____

5. _____

Fate le domande e rispondete. Poi, scrivete il dialogo. *(With a partner, ask the question or give the answer. Then, write the dialogue.)*

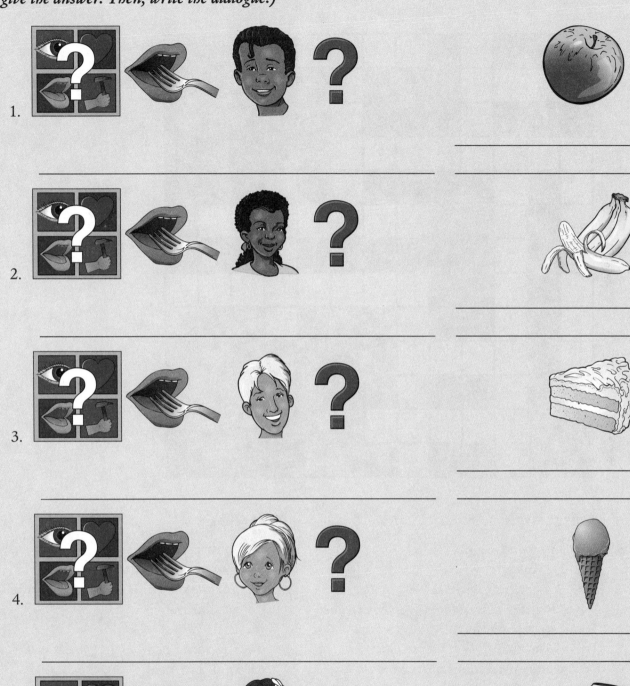

Il cruciverba

Orizzontale

2. I'm thirsty. = *Ho* _____.
4. I'm hungry. = *Ho* _____.
5. dinner time wish: *Buon* _____!
8. Quality with taste! = _____ *con sapore!*
9. called *patate* in Italy
10. eggs
11. what is placed on *un piattino*

Verticale

1. to drink
3. what is set for meals
5. a fruit, the color of which has a similar name
6. ham
7. shopping list = *la* _____ *della spesa*
9. mid-day meal

Unit 10

L'arte

Art

Three Great Artists

Ginevra de' Benci

(oil on panel, 1474) by Leonardo da Vinci

National Gallery of Art, Washington, D.C.
Ailsa Mellon Bruce Fund

Leonardo da Vinci is one of the most famous artists in the western hemisphere. He was born in 1452 in the small village of Anchiano. Like Albrecht Dürer in Germany, Leonardo lived in the age of the Renaissance— a time of renewed interest in the humanities, science, and exploration. Like Dürer, he preferred classical lines, natural proportions, and realistic portrayals based on observation and measurement. In fact, he wrote the book *Treatise on Painting* about the relationship between art and science.

Leonardo's projects reflected his many interests and talents. He enjoyed geometry, geology, physics, machinery, anatomy, and botany. The fresco (wall painting) of *The Last Supper* is a model of perspective with Christ as the central figure. In the portrait *Mona Lisa*, Leonardo used a shadowy effect. By combining light and shadow he gave his subject both a natural or real appearance and an unreal one.

Other projects included the portrait *Ginevra de' Benci*, many scientific sketches and even a huge horse. (This clay horse was supposed to be bronzed as a sculpture, but it was destroyed by French invaders in 1499. Five hundred years later, American sculptor Charles Dent started to fulfill Leonardo's plan to create the statue. After his death another American sculptor, Nina Akamu, created the 24-foot tall horse and it was presented to the city of Milan in 1999.)

The Horse

Original by Leonardo da Vinci

Milan, Italy

Kaiser Karl V
(oil on canvas, 1548) by Titian

Alte Pinakothek, Muchen

The Vendramin Family
(oil on canvas, 1543–47) by Titian

The National Gallery, London

While in Italy, Leonardo worked as a painter, a draftsman, a sculptor, an architect, and a military engineer. His last employment was in France as a designer of court pageantries for King Francis I. He died in France in 1519.

Born in 1487 in a small village north of Venice, **Tiziano (Titian)** grew up to be a very popular and innovative artist. His real name was **Tiziano Vecellio**. He had little interest in the artistic ideals of the Renaissance and developed his own personal style emphasizing color and individual expression. Titian spent most of his life in Venice doing portraits for wealthy clients. He also worked in Augsburg at the Habsburg court where he was official court painter. Titian influenced other artisits such as Velazquez, El Greco, and Rubens. Titian died of the plague in 1576.

The portrait *Kaiser Karl V (Charles V)* shows an imposing figure placed amid the contrasts of setting, color, and mood: the room versus the look of a tired and patient man.

In the portrait *The Vendramin Family,* the viewer's attention is divided between the adults and the children. The men show reverence for the shrine while the children seem occupied with their own thoughts. The artist allows the individual expression of the people to minimize the importance of the shrine.

Canaletto, or **Giovanni Antonio Canal (Canale)**, was born in Venice in 1697. Like his father, he became a stage decorator. He painted scenery for operas, stage productions, and even for the Carnival in 1719 and 1720. About the time when the Flemish landscape artists were visiting Rome, Canaletto turned his attention to panoramas. He soon perfected his skill at creating cityscapes, or large views of Venice, Rome, and London. He enjoyed much popularity in Italy and England. He died in Venice in 1768.

Canaletto's art is characterized as linear, clear, and realistic. One painting called *The Stonemason's Yard* shows the lifestyle of a simple laborer. Others show magificient buildings and the lifestyle of wealthier people.

The Stonemason's Yard
(oil on canvas, 1727–28) by Canaletto

The National Gallery, London

A Regatta on the Grand Canal
(oil on canvas, 1740) by Canaletto

The National Gallery, London

Le attività

A Chi è? *(Who is it?)*

1. English art historians call this person Titian. What is Titian's full name in Italian?

   _____

2. Like Titian, this artist is commonly called by his first name. What is this name?

   _____

3. This artist used a diminutive or "mini" version of his famous father's name. What did he call himself?

   _____

B Quale artista? *Identify the Italian artist whose works reveal:*

1. bright colors

   _____

2. realistic views of urban life

   _____

3. classical proportions

   _____

C Fai accoppiare gli oggetti del gruppo B con quelli del gruppo A. *Match the groups.*

A	B
1. _____ Venice	A. influenced by Titian
2. _____ *The Last Supper*	B. where Canaletto lived for a time
3. _____ Velazquez, El Greco, and Rubens	C. wall painting
4. _____ *The Stonemason's Yard*	D. where Tiziano worked as a court painter
5. _____ Augsburg	E. depicts the lifestyle of a simple laborer

D **Completa le analogie.**

1. Leonardo da Vinci: Italy   = Albrecht Dürer: _____

2. Tiziano: portraits   = _____: panoramas

3. *Mona Lisa:* _____ = *Kaiser Karl V*: Tiziano

4. Anchiano: _____ = Venice: Canaletto

5. Individual style: Tiziano   = _____: Leonardo da Vinci

E **Fai corrispondere il nome all' illustrazione.** *(Match the picture cue to the associated artist's name.)*

1. _____ Tiziano   A.

2. _____ Canaletto   B.

3. _____ Leonardo da Vinci   C.

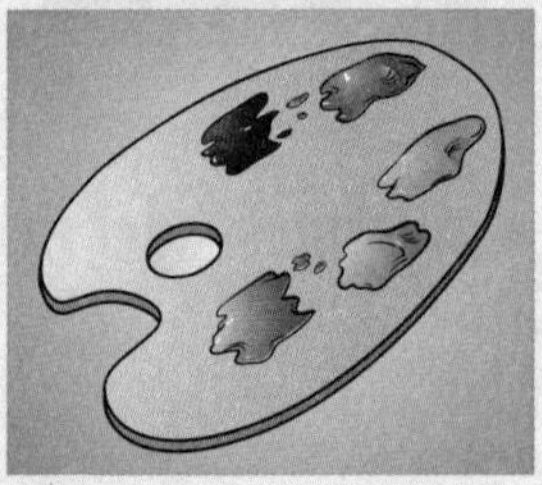

F **Quale artista sarebbe?** *Which artist would most likely be . . .*

1. . . . happy to talk with scientists and philosophers?

_____

2. . . . eager to show you the sights of Rome or Venice?

_____

3. . . . pleased to experiment with new colors?

_____

G **Secondo te?** *In your opinion . . .*

1. . . . whose work might hang in a mayor's office?

_____

2. . . . whose work would appeal to someone who wants a portrait done?

_____

3. . . . whose work might be included in a technical manual about bridges, pulleys, and cannons?

_____

H **Quale quadro ti piace?** *Which of the pictures in this unit do you like best? Who created this masterpiece? State in your own words what the picture is about and why you like it.*

_____

_____

_____

I **Completa correttamente ogni frase in inglese.**

1. Both Tiziano and Leonardo painted _____ of people.

2. Canaletto liked to paint large views of _____.

3. Leonardo da Vinci sketched and painted very _____.

J **Tocca a te!** Choose an object or animal that you have learned the name for in this book, for example, a rabbit. On a sheet of paper or on the board, make your rabbit in two different styles: Classical and Modern (Expressionistic, Abstract, or Avant-garde). Label each as follows: *È un coniglio.* Let the class see your drawings and vote twice: first on artistic style (which drawing is Classical and which one is Modern), and second on personal preference (which one the class prefers). Announce in Italian that you are an artist!

Proverbio

" Impara l'arte e
mettila da parte.
Learn art and keep
it forever. "

Lingua viva!

Al Museo di Capodimonte, dal 24 marzo, una mostra racconta i protagonisti delle corti europee del '500, ritratti da Tiziano e compagni

Napoli
Tiziano e il potere

Primo pittore della Repubblica di Venezia dal 1516, lavorò nelle diverse corti europee, chiamato da Alfonso I d'Este a Ferrara, poi a Mantova per i Gonzaga e ad Urbino. Nel 1542 inizia a collaborare con papa Paolo III e la famiglia Farnese, trasferendosi a Roma per un anno, dal 1545. Diventerà quindi il pittore prediletto dell'imperatore Carlo V e del figlio Filippo II, lavorando intensamente fino alla morte, avvenuta nell'agosto del 1576. ■

Le informazioni sulla mostra

Tiziano e il ritratto di corte del Cinquecento da Raffaello ai Carracci
La mostra è aperta dal 24 marzo al 4 giugno; tutti i giorni dalle 8.30 alle 19.30; mercoledì chiuso.
Info e prenotazioni: 848800288. Ingresso: Mostra + Museo 10 euro; ridotto 5 euro.
Il percorso espositivo comprende le opere della collezione Farnese del Museo Capodimonte oltre ad altri 30 ritratti di Tiziano e altri 50 dipinti di artisti a lui contemporanei, da Raffaello a Pontormo, da Tintoretto a Moroni, da Sebastiano del Piombo a Ludovico Carracci.

Tutto Antonello

La cosa straordinaria sarà vedere riunite, per la prima volta in Italia, praticamente tutte le opere conosciute oggi di Antonello da Messina: una quarantina di dipinti sparsi in diversi musei italiani e stranieri. Ma la mostra dedicata al maestro del Quattrocento alle Scuderie del Quirinale presenterà anche molte novità sul fronte degli studi, grazie ad una campagna di indagini con moderne tecnologie all'infrarosso che ha "messo a nudo" tutti i dipinti. Tornano per l'occasione la "Madonna col Bambino" e il "San Gerolamo nello studio" dalla National Gallery di Londra, il "San Sebastiano" da Anversa e il "Cristo alla Colonna" dal Louvre, affiancati a dipinti presenti in musei italiani come la "Vergine annunciata" di Palermo. Le opere dell'artista siciliano si confrontano poi con quelle di altri artisti quali Jan van Eyck, Giovanni Bellini, Alvise Vivarini, Francesco Laurana.

ANTONELLO DA MESSINA
Roma Scuderie del Quirinale
Dal 18 marzo al 18 giugno
Tel. 06 39967500

K **Look at the top clippings and answer the following questions.**

1. Name the painter whose works are shown.

   _____

2. He died in 1576; can you tell in which month?

   _____

3. The exhibit is open every day except for one, which one?

   _____

4. How much does it cost to enter the museum and the exhibit?

   _____

5. The word *ridotto* means reduced and refers to a students, children, or senior citizens discount. How much is the discounted price?

   _____

6. In which Italian city is the exhibit presented?

   _____

L **Look at the bottom clipping and answer the following questions.**

1. What is Antonello's last name?

   _____

2. Can you tell from his last name where he is from?

   _____

3. In which century did he live?

   _____

4. Which Italian city is hosting the exhibit?

   _____

5. What are the dates of the exhibit?

   _____

Symtalk

M Scrivi nello spazio la parola giusta in italiano. *(In the space, write the correct word in Italian.)*

1. _____
2. _____
3. _____
4. _____
5. _____
6. _____
7. _____
8. _____

N Dì le frasi, poi scrivile in italiano. *(Say the sentences, then write them in Italian.)*

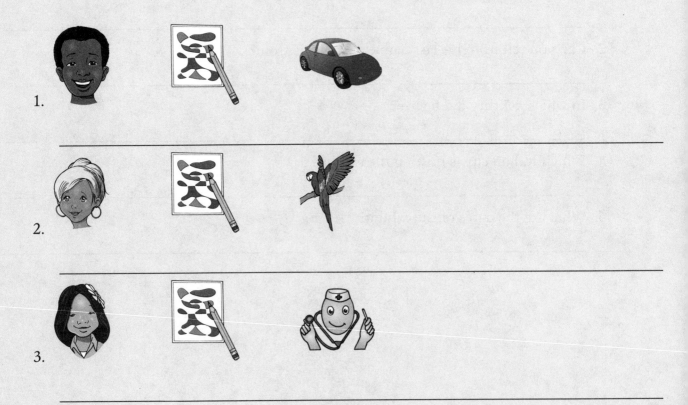

1. _____

2. _____

3. _____

4.

5.

O Fate le domande e rispondete. Poi, scrivete il dialogo. *(With a partner, ask the question or give the answer. Then, write the dialogue.)*

1.

2.

3.

4.

Il cruciverba

Orizzontale

3. picture of one person or several people
6. *The Stonemason's* ____
8. *Mona* ____
9. city painted by Canaletto
10. woman who posed for Leonardo: *de'*____
11. one of Leonardo's interests

Verticale

1. city know for its Grand Canal
2. man who posed for Tiziano: ____ V
3. large view of a city or land area
4. cultural age in which Leonardo lived
5. Tiziano's last name
7. artist who enjoyed science

Unit 11

Il corpo e la salute
Body and Health

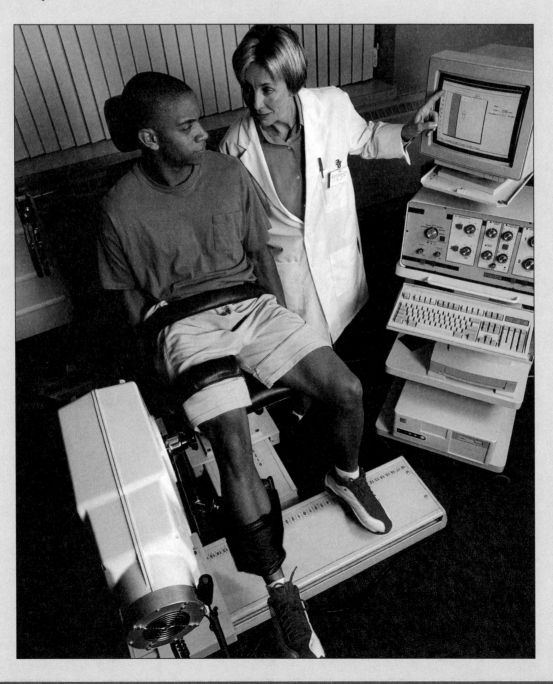

Il vocabolario

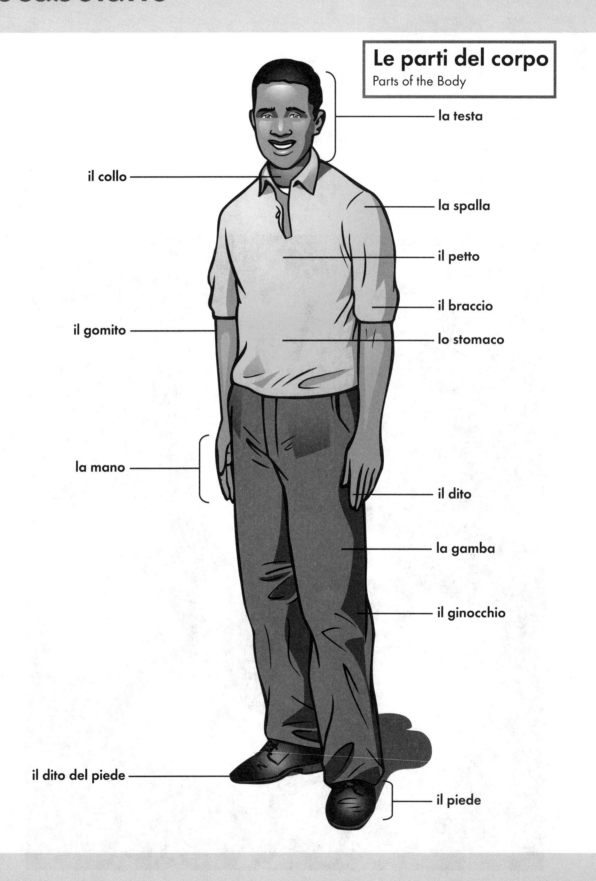

Le parti del corpo
Parts of the Body

- la testa
- il collo
- la spalla
- il petto
- il braccio
- il gomito
- lo stomaco
- la mano
- il dito
- la gamba
- il ginocchio
- il dito del piede
- il piede

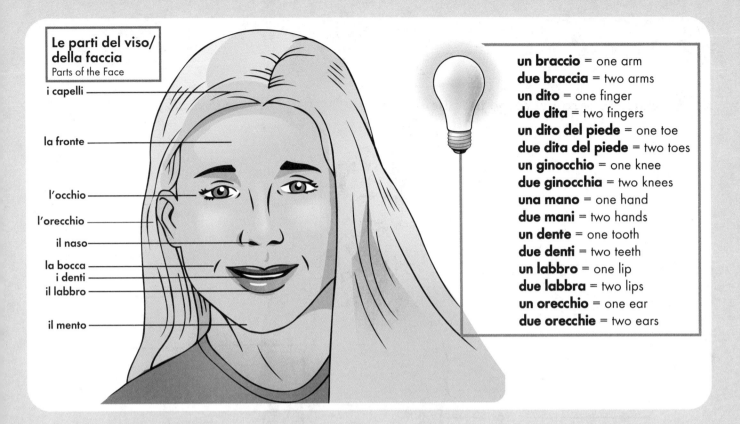

Le parti del viso/ della faccia
Parts of the Face

i capelli
la fronte
l'occhio
l'orecchio
il naso
la bocca
i denti
il labbro
il mento

un braccio = one arm
due braccia = two arms
un dito = one finger
due dita = two fingers
un dito del piede = one toe
due dita del piede = two toes
un ginocchio = one knee
due ginocchia = two knees
una mano = one hand
due mani = two hands
un dente = one tooth
due denti = two teeth
un labbro = one lip
due labbra = two lips
un orecchio = one ear
due orecchie = two ears

Extra Vocabolario

la salute health	**bene** well	**contento/a; allegro/a** happy	**malato** sick, ill	**male** bad	**sano** healthy	**triste** sad

UMBERTO: **Ciao, Lucia, come stai?**
Hi, Lucia! How are you?

LUCIA: **Non sto bene. Mi sento male.**
I'm not doing well. I feel bad.

ETTORE: **Lavori molto?**
Are you working a lot?

OTTAVIANO: **No, studio per un esame.**
No, I'm studying for a test.

LARA: **Che cos'hai?/Che c'è?**
What's the matter?

DAVIDE: **Ho mal di testa.**
I've got a headache.

CARLO: **Gianna è malata oggi?**
Is Gianna sick today?

TEO: **Sì. Ha l'influenza.**
Yes. She has the flu.

ALBERTO: **Come ti senti?/Come stai?**
How do you feel?

MARÍA: **Mi sento bene./Sto bene.**
I'm feeling well.

NICOLA: **Sei triste, Paola?**
Are you sad, Paola?

PAOLA: **No. Sono allegra!**
No. I'm happy!

Le attività

A **Marca le parti del corpo in italiano, per favore.** *(Label parts of the body.)*

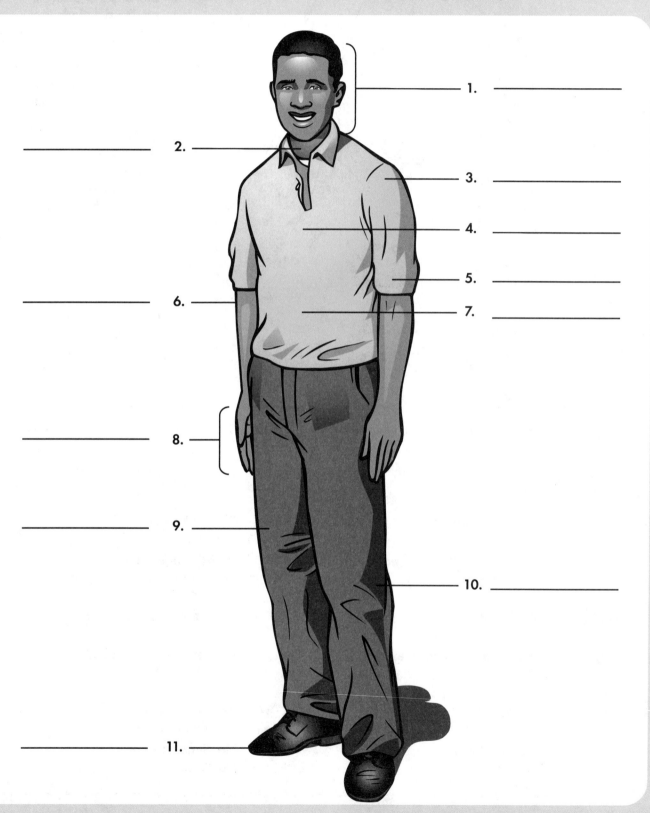

1. _____

2. _____

3. _____

4. _____

5. _____

6. _____

7. _____

8. _____

9. _____

10. _____

11. _____

Il corpo e la salute

B Marca le parti della faccia in italiano. *(Label the parts of the face.)*

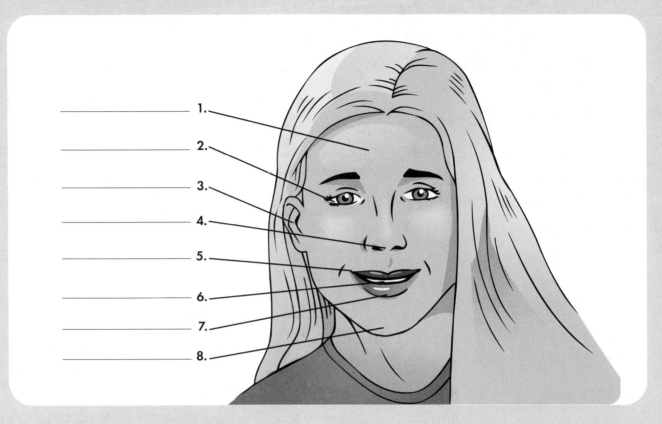

1. _____
2. _____
3. _____
4. _____
5. _____
6. _____
7. _____
8. _____

C Completa ogni frase in italiano. *(Complete each sentence in Italian.)*

1. We see with our _____.

2. To speak I open my _____.

3. An _____ is necessary to hear.

4. You hold your pen in your _____.

5. Your _____ are needed to bite and chew food.

6. One _____ has five toes.

7. We use the _____ to smell a rose.

8. We play the guitar with our _____.

9. The "funny bone" is located on the _____.

10. If you eat too much, your _____ will hurt.

D **I verbi.** *What do you do with your senses? Guess the meaning of the italicized verbs. If you know the nouns, then you can easily figure out the verbs!*

1. Io *parlo* con la bocca. _____

2. Io *tocco* con le dita. _____

3. Io *vedo* con gli occhi. _____

4. Io *sento* con le orecchie. _____

5. Io *sento il profumo* con il naso. _____

E **Completa i dialoghi in italiano.** *(Complete the dialogues in Italian.)*

1. LUIGI: Come ti senti, Marta?

   MARTA: Mi sento _____. *(bad)*

2. GIAN CARLO: Come stai, Enrico?

   ENRICO: Sto _____. *(well)*

3. DIANA: Rosa ha l'influenza?

   ALESSIA: Sì, è _____. *(sick)*

4. BIANCA: Sei triste?

   LEONARDO: No, sono _____. *(happy)*

F **Identifica le parti del corpo in italiano.** *Name the part of the body associated with each illustration.*

1. _____

2. _____

3. _____

4. _____

5. _____

6. _____

7. _____

8.  _____

9.  _____

10.  _____

G **Quale attività usa quale parte del corpo?** *Match each part of the body to the activity associated with it.*

A	B
1. _____ la mano	A. running
2. _____ il piede	B. smelling
3. _____ gli occhi	C. carrying
4. _____ il naso	D. listening
5. _____ le orecchie	E. seeing
6. _____ lo stomaco	F. thinking
7. _____ la bocca	G. digesting
8. _____ il braccio	H. writing
9. _____ la testa	I. touching
10. _____ il dito	J. speaking

H **Leggi il brano. Scegli le risposte giuste.** *(Read the passage. Choose the correct answers.)*

> Mi chiamo Alessia. Ho dieci anni. Sto bene e sono sana. *Penso con* la testa. Parlo italiano con la bocca. Scrivo con la mano e *cammino* a scuola con i piedi e le gambe. Ammiro i quadri di Leonardo Da Vinci con gli occhi. *Sento il profumo* dei fiori nel giardino con il naso. *Mastico* il cibo con i denti. Il corpo è meraviglioso, non è vero?

con	with	**(Io) cammino**	I walk	**(Io) mastico**	I chew
(Io) penso	I think	**(Io) sento/il profumo**	I smell		

1. Alessia è _____.
   A. una ragazza
   B. un uomo
   C. un ragazzo
   D. una donna

2. Alessia ha _____ anni.
   A. undici
   B. nove
   C. dodici
   D. dieci

3. Alessia parla con _____.
   A. la mano
   B. la gamba
   C. la bocca
   D. l'orecchio

4. Con le gambe, Alessia _____.
   A. cammina a scuola
   B. scrive a Pietro
   C. ammira i quadri di Botticelli
   D. sente il profumo dei fiori

5. Alessia è molto _____.
   A. triste
   B. allegra
   C. scontenta
   D. malata

I **Parliamo!** Locate ten parts of the body. Ask your classmate in Italian where a part of the body is. Your classmate will point to his/her part. Take turns until you have found and located all ten parts.

> **Modello:** A: Dov'è il naso? *(Where is the nose?)*
> B: Ecco il naso. *(Here is the nose.)*

J **Tocca a te!** Find magazine pictures showing healthy, active, and happy people and other pictures of people looking sick or unhappy. Paste these pictures on a poster and write a short description of each one. For example, under a picture of a girl with a cold, write *È malata* or *Ha l'influenza*. Under the picture of a boy playing, write *È allegro*.

Look at the clippings and answer the following questions.

1. Can you find the Italian word for health?

   _____

2. What do you think *bellezza* means?_____

3. The word *bene* means "well," and the word *essere* means "being." Can you find the Italian word for "wellbeing"? _____

4. The word *città* means city; what do you think the word *cittadini* means?

   _____

5. Can you guess what *invalidità* means?

   _____

L **Look at the ad for health center "Essere benessere" and answer the following questions.**

1. How much is a session at the center? _____

2. What do you think *massaggio* means? _____

3. What do you think *prenotazioni* means? _____

Proverbio

" Chi va piano, va
sano e va lontano.
Easy does it. "

Symtalk

M Scrivi nello spazio la parola giusta in italiano. *(In the space, write the correct word in Italian.)*

1. _____ 2. _____ 3. _____ 4. _____

5. _____ 6. _____ 7. _____

N Dì le frasi, poi scrivile in italiano. *(Say the sentences then write them in Italian.)*

1. _____

2. _____

3. _____

4. _____

5.

_____

O **Fate le domande e rispondete. Poi, scrivete il dialogo.** *(With a partner, ask the question or give the answer. Then, write the dialogue.)*

1.

_____

2.

_____

3.

_____

4.

_____

Il cruciverba

Orizzontale

2. Sto ____. Sono triste.
4. La ____ è molto importante! *(health)*
5. Uso la ____ per scrivere.
10. ____ stai?
11. Uso gli ____ per vedere.
12. Mi fa male la ____. *(headache)*
13. Uso i ____ per camminare a casa.

Verticale

1. Io non sto ____. Sono malata.
2. Gianna non sta bene oggi. È ____.
3. Giorgio non è triste. È ____.
6. Uso le ____ per ascoltare.
7. Uso la ____ per parlare.
8. Che cos' ____?
9. Uso i ____ per mangiare.

Unit 12

I vestiti

Clothing

Il vocabolario

La moda

il maglione/
il golf

il pigiama

il completo/l'abito

la camicia

la cravatta

il fazzoletto

la giacca

i pantaloni

le scarpe　　i calzini　　i guanti

il vestito/
l'abito

il pigiama

il cappello

la camicetta
di seta

la cintura

la gonna

l'accappatoio/
la vestaglia

le scarpe coi
tacchi alti

le scarpe
da tennis

GIANNI: **Che cosa porti?**
What are you wearing?

FILIPPO: **Porto il mio nuovo completo.**
I'm wearing my new suit.

GIANNI: **Perchè?**
Why?

FILIPPO: **Vado ad un concerto stasera.**
I'm going to a concert this evening.

ANDREA: **Vado in giardino.**
I'm going out into the yard.

SARA: **Aspettami. Vengo con te. Ma
prima, cerco la mia giacca.**
Wait for me. I'm coming with you. But
first, I'm going to look for my jacket.

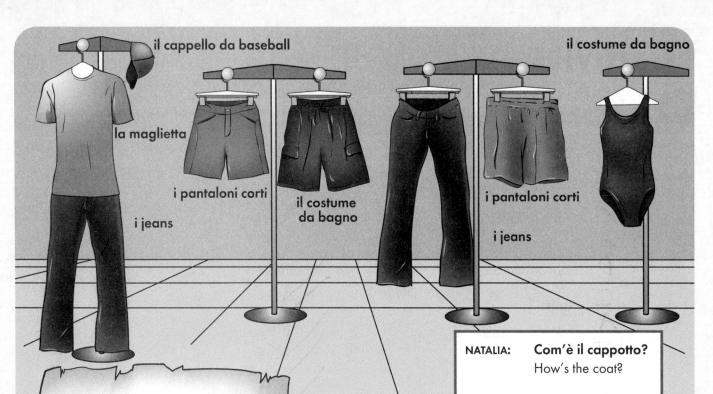

il cappello da baseball

la maglietta

i pantaloni corti

i jeans

il costume
da bagno

i pantaloni corti

i jeans

il costume da bagno

NATALIA: **Com'è il cappotto?**
How's the coat?

GINO: **È molto bello.**
It's very pretty.

ORLANDO: **Che cosa fai, Margherita?**
What are you doing, Margherita?

MARGHERITA: **Faccio la valigia.**
I'm packing my suitcase.

ORLANDO: **Perchè?**
Why?

MARGHERITA: **Perchè vado a Torino fra poco.**
I'm traveling to Torino soon.

ORLANDO: **Non dimenticare i tuoi vestiti da sci.**
Don't forget your ski clothing.

Margherita

La vacanza invernale
Winter vacation

Torino - Gennaio
Torino - January

2 vestiti	*3 camicie*
3 cappelli	*2 camicette*
1 pigiama	*1 gonna*
2 cinture	*1 cappotto*
3 fazzoletti	*dei calzini*
1 giacca	*le scarpe*
1 maglione	*i guanti*
3 paia di pantaloni	

- Use *bella* to describe a singular feminine-gender word, *La giacca è bella.*
- Use *bello* to describe a singular masculine-gender word, *Il cappotto è bello.*

Le attività

A **Metti insieme le parole italiane con le parole inglesi.** *(Match the Italian and the English words.)*

	A		B
1. E	la gonna	A.	handkerchief
2. F	la cintura	B.	jacket
3. G	i pantaloni	C.	coat
4. D	la cravatta	D.	tie
5. I	i guanti	E.	skirt
6. A	il fazzoletto	F.	belt
7. J	l'accappatoio	G.	pants
8. ___	il cappotto	H.	shoes
9. H	le scarpe	I.	gloves
10. C	la giacca	J.	bathrobe
11. L	il costume da bagno	K.	baseball cap
12. K	il cappello da baseball	L.	bathing suit

B **Che cosa porti?** *(What do you wear?)* **Rispondi in italiano.**

1. . . . to school?

_____

2. . . . to a symphony concert?

_____

3. . . . to bed?

_____

4. . . . in cool weather?

_____

5. . . . in cold weather?

_____

6. . . . to a swimming pool?

_____

C **Completa le analogie.**

1. i guanti: le mani = ___*le scarpe*___ : i piedi

2. _____ : la gonna = la camicia: i pantaloni

3. la vestaglia: il pigiama = il cappotto: _____

4. la cravatta: la camicia = ___*le scarpe*___ : i pantaloni

D **Completa ogni frase con la parola italiana.** *(Complete each sentence with the Italian word for the picture.)*

1. Porto un _____ .

2. Porto un _____ .

3. Porto un _____ .

4.

Porto una _____

e una _____.

5.

Porto un _____

e una _____.

E **Scrivi il senso in inglese.** *(Write the meaning in English.)*

1. portare _____

2. Lui/Lei porta _____

3. Io porto _____

4. Tu porti _____

F Fai la lista in italiano. *(List the required number of items for each category.)*

outdoor clothing (4)

1. _____
2. _____
3. _____
4. _____

accessories (3)

5. _____
6. _____
7. _____

footwear (3)

8. _____
9. _____
10. _____

sleepwear (1)

11. _____

G Scegli la parola corretta per poter completare la frase. *(Choose the correct word in order to complete the sentence.)*

1. Faccio _____.
   A. la valigia
   B. la moda degli uomini
   C. il mio giardino
   D. le scarpe

2. Tu porti _____.
   A. la porta
   B. la tua salute
   C. l'aula
   D. una gonna e una camicetta

3. Non dimenticare di portare _____.
   A. il giardino
   B. i tuoi guanti
   C. Aosta
   D. le montagne

4. Vado a cercare una giacca perchè _____.
   A. aspettami
   B. è la mia giacca
   C. vado in giardino
   D. sto portando una giacca

5. Porto un nuovo completo perchè _____.
   A. viaggio in montagna tra poco
   B. ho una bella cravatta
   C. vado ad un concerto stasera
   D. faccio la valigia

6. Il cappotto è _____.
   A. un cappello da baseball
   B. una maglietta
   C. stasera
   D. bello

Leggi il brano. Scegli le risposte corrette. *(Read the passage. Select the correct answers.)*

> Margherita va in vacanza con la sua famiglia. Visita Torino, una città al nord
> dell'Italia. *Fa la sua valigia. Porta solo i suoi* vestiti *invernali*. Porta due paia di
> pantaloni, due maglioni, un vestito, una gonna, una camicetta e una giacca. Lei
> ha *già tutti* i vestiti *adatti* per il viaggio. Margherita è allegra!

va in vacanza	is going on vacation
Fa la sua valigia.	She is packing her suitcase.
Porta solo	she is only bringing
invernali	for winter
adatti	right, suitable
i suoi	her
già	already
tutti	all

1. Chi va in vacanza?
   A. vacanza
   B. nord
   C. Torino
   D. Margherita

2. Che cosa mette nella sua valigia?
   A. Torino
   B. la sua famiglia
   C. Margherita
   D. i vestiti invernali

3. Quante paia di pantaloni porta
   Margherita?
   A. quattro
   B. tre
   C. due
   D. uno

4. Porta un vestito nella valigia?
   A. Sì, porta un vestito.
   B. No, ne porta due.
   C. No, ne porta tre.
   B. No, non porta un vestito.

Che cos'altro deve portare a Torino? *In your opinion, what other articles of clothing should Margherita take along for the cold winter days of January in Torino? Answer in Italian.*

_____

_____

_____

_____

_____

J Parliamo! Ask your speaking partner: What are you wearing today? *(Che cosa porti oggi?)* He/she should answer with: *Porto . . .* and then name an article of clothing. Then reverse roles. Be sure to mention at least three items each.

K Tocca a te! Time yourselves. Set a stopwatch for twenty seconds. Your partner will choose a category of clothing, such as casual clothes. If you can correctly name all the items in that category, give yourself a gold star. If you can't, or if the clock beats you, your partner takes over. This time, you select a category, and he/she will answer. Continue until all the categories are covered: casual clothes, outdoor cold weather clothes, bedtime clothes, accessories, and clothes for special occasions. The person with the most gold stars wins.

tempo**libero**mobility

Aria di primavera

1 Cinture È l'accessorio del momento, per dare un tocco originale ad un semplice jeans o alla gonna più elegante. Supercolorate quelle proposte da Benetton con effetto rettile stampato (24,90 euro). **2 Polo** Stile optical in colori pastello per la versione più sbarazzina del modello classico proposto da Benetton, che così entra nelle valigie delle più giovani (35,90 euro). **3 Ciabattine** Indossarli sarà un po' come camminare su atolli tropicali, i sandali della collezione Oceano, con l'allegro decoro di fiori in stoffa (prezzo su richiesta: tel. 02 4223329). **4 Yoga Bag wih Mat** I benefici dello yoga derivano da una pratica costante? La Nike propone una comoda borsa per trasportare ovunque il tappetino e allenare l'armonia anche in viaggio (55 euro). **5 Bikini** Per chi già rincorre i primi raggi di sole o da esibire a bordo piscina il costume Congo, della nuova collezione Calzedonia, dall'aria "baby" (45,90 euro). **6 Occhiali da sole** Voglia di anni '70 con il modello di Trussardi by Visibilia che ripropone la tradizionale goccia in metallo ma con dettagli in pelle (133 euro). **7 T-shirt** Le teen-ager da anni ne hanno fatto un simbolo, un marchio da indossare su borse, cinture ma soprattutto su pratiche magliette. Per sentirsi sempre "cool" (info: www.bluedistribution.it; 36 euro). **8 Beauty** Per combattere le rughe Chanel presenta il nuovo programma Micro Solutions, con un gel da applicare con un fissatore e uno strumento per il massaggio che si portano comodamente nella trousse (182 euro). **9 Borsa mare** Fantasia multicolor e tessuto impermeabile per la borsa di Gallo, pensata per la spiaggia ma adatta pure per le scampagnate (100 euro). **10 Salviette dei piccoli** Per il cambio dei pannolini, ma anche per pulire viso, corpo e manine quando mancano acqua e sapone. L'Erbolario (4,50 euro). **11 Pallone da calcio** In omaggio ai Mondiali Bruno Cucinelli propone un pallone regolamentare rivestito di cachemire. In perfetto abbinamento alla "borsa da diligenza" e alla sacca in tela (380, 2400, 600 euro).

riflessi 77

Look at the clippings and answer the following questions.

1. What is the season featured in this article?

   Primavera

2. Find the Italian word for the following items.
   A. Soccer ball *Pallone*
   B. Belts *Cinturi*
   C. Sunglasses *Occhiali da sole*

 Look at the clipping and answer the following questions.

1. How much does a belt cost?

   ~~€~~ *24.90 Euro*

2. If I buy two pairs of sunglasses, how much do I pay?

   ~~€~~ *266*

3. What do you think *ciabattine* means if the word *ciabatte* means "slippers"?

4. How much does a *Borsa Mare* cost? Based on the fact that *mare* means "sea," what kind of items are you likely to carry in this bag?

   € 100

5. What is the name for "wipes" in Italian?

   Salviette dei piccoli

Proverbio

" **L'abito non fa il monaco.**

Don't judge a book by it's cover. "

Symtalk

N Scrivi nello spazio la parola giusta in italiano. *(In the space, write the correct word in Italian.)*

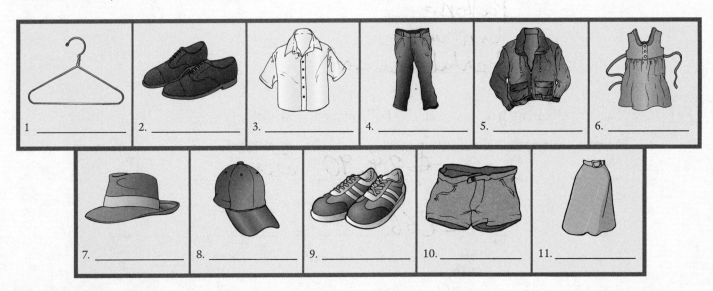

1. _____ 2. _____ 3. _____ 4. _____ 5. _____ 6. _____

7. _____ 8. _____ 9. _____ 10. _____ 11. _____

O Dì le frasi, poi scrivile in italiano. *(Say the sentences, then write them in Italian.)*

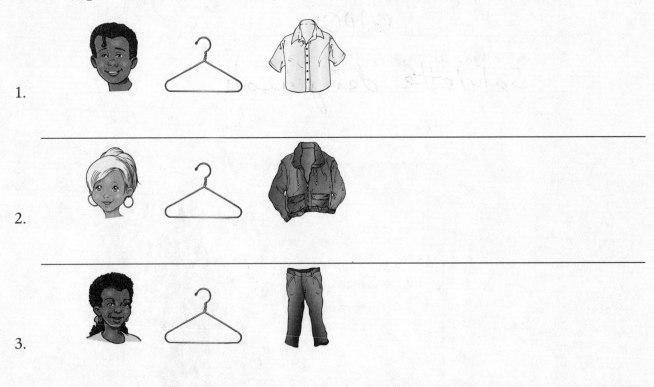

1.

_____

2.

_____

3.

_____

4.

_____

P **Fate le domande e rispondete. Poi, scrivete il dialogo.** *(With a partner, ask the question or give the answer. Then, write the dialogue.)*

1.

                                                  No, _____

_____

2.

                                                  No, _____

_____

3.

                                                  No, _____

_____

4.

                                                  No, _____

_____

Il cruciverba

For this crossword puzzle, use a form of the definite article *(the)* before each word.

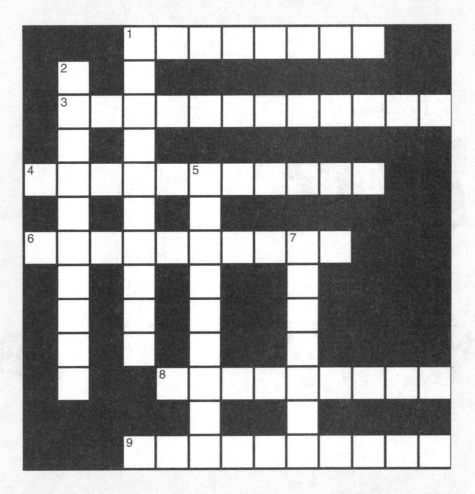

Orizzontale

1. feet protectors
3. worn after a bath
4. often worn with a skirt
6. head protector
8. holds up pants/trousers
9. long pants, trousers or slacks

Verticale

1. neckwear
2. worn when a jacket is too warm
5. sleepwear
7. often worn with a blouse

Unit 13

L'ora e i colori
Time and Colors

Vocabolario

Che ore sono?/Che ora è?
What time is it?

È l'una e mezza.   **Sono le tre.**   **Sono le dieci meno un quarto.**   **È mezzogiorno.**

A che ora . . . ?
At what time . . . ?

Alle due e cinque.   **Alle sette e un quarto.**   **Alle undici e cinquantacinque./A mezzogiorno meno cinque.**   **A Mezzanotte.**

- Transportation in Europe operates on official time, which is on a twenty-four hour basis. Official time is often used by school, radio and television stations, and movie theaters.

- *È* is used with *mezzogiorno* (noon) and *mezzanotte* (midnight). It is also used with the number one, **È l'una.** (It's one o'clock.) *Sono* is used with all other numbers, **Sono le due.** (It's two o'clock.)

Di che colore è. . .?
What color is. . .?

È. . .
It is. . .

Di che colore sono. . .?
What color(s) are. . .?

Sono. . .
They are. . .

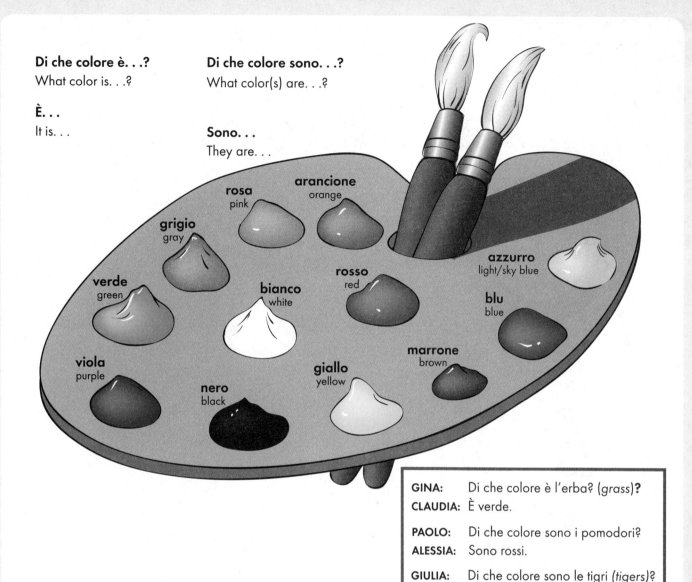

rosa pink
arancione orange
grigio gray
azzurro light/sky blue
verde green
bianco white
rosso red
blu blue
viola purple
nero black
giallo yellow
marrone brown

GINA:	Di che colore è l'erba? (*grass*)**?**
CLAUDIA:	È verde.
PAOLO:	Di che colore sono i pomodori?
ALESSIA:	Sono rossi.
GIULIA:	Di che colore sono le tigri (*tigers*)?
ANDREA:	Sono arancioni e nere.

- ***Rosa, blu,*** and ***viola*** are invariable adjectives. They do not change to agree in gender and number with the noun they are modifying.

  *Il maglione è **rosa**. Le camicie sono **rosa**.*

- The adjectives ***marrone*** and ***arancione*** can be either invariable, or act as adjectives ending in "e" like ***verde***. Adjectives ending in "e" have one ending for singular nouns, both masculine and feminine, and one ending for plural nouns.

  *Il maglione è **verde**. La gonna è **verde**.*
  *I vestiti sono **verdi**. Le camicie sono **verdi**.*

- Adjectives ending in "o" have four endings to help them agree with the nouns they modify.

  *Il maglione è **azzurro**. La gonna è **azzurra**.*
  *I vestiti sono **azzurri**. Le camicie sono **azzurre**.*

Le attività

A *Che ore sono?* **Listen as your teacher says a time. Find the clock that shows that time, and label it number 1. Then your teacher will express another time. Mark the clock expressing that time as number 2. Continue until all eight clocks are numbered.**

1. _____

2. _____

3. _____

4. _____

       L'ora e i colori

5. _____

6. _____

7. _____

8. _____

B Completa le frasi in italiano. *(Complete the sentences in Italian.)*

1. Light red is called _rosa_.
2. A bluebird or robin's egg is _azurro_.
3. Chocolate is _marrone_.
4. A lemon is _giallo_.
5. In the summer, a leaf is _verde_.
6. Tar is _nero_.
7. The color _arancione_ is the color of a pumpkin.
8. The sky on a very cloudy day looks _grigio_.
9. A marshmallow is _bianco_.
10. A strawberry is _rosso_.

C Scrivi in italiano. *(Write in Italian.)*

1. At seven o'clock. _Sono le sette_
2. It's half past one. _È l'una e mezze_
3. At 8:10. _____
4. It's 2:40. _____
5. At twenty past three. _Sono le tre e venti_

D What color are they? *(Di che colore sono?)* **Match the items in column *A* with the colors in column *B*.**

A   B

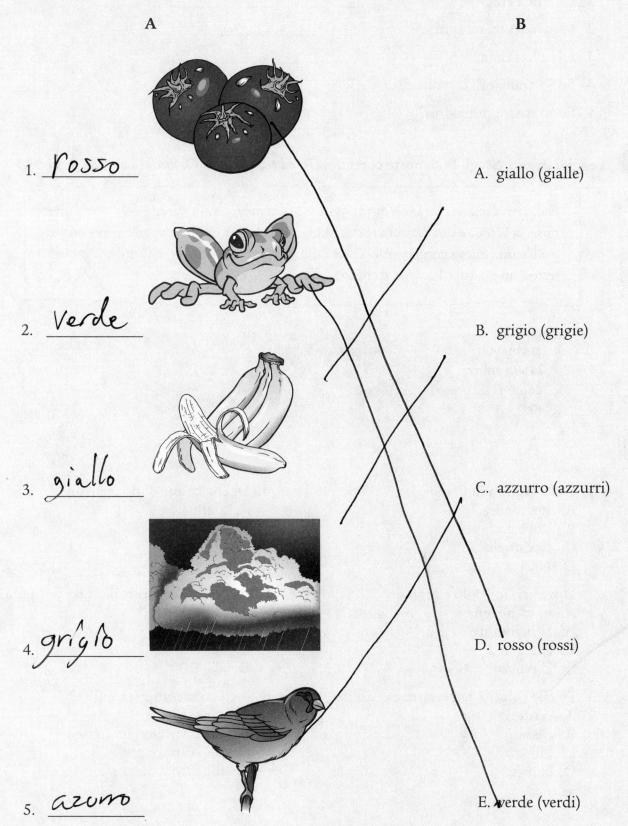

1. _rosso_

2. _verde_

3. _giallo_

4. _grigio_

5. _azurro_

A. giallo (gialle)

B. grigio (grigie)

C. azzurro (azzurri)

D. rosso (rossi)

E. verde (verdi)

E Rispondi con "sì" o "no". (*Answer with "yes" or "no."*)

1. È verde l'erba?   _____

2. Sono azzurri gli spinaci?   _____

3. È giallo l'elefante?   _____

4. Sono arancioni le banane?   _____

5. Sono rossi i pomodori?   _____

F Leggi il brano. Scegli le risposte corrette. (*Read the passage. Choose the correct answers.*)

Paolo va *al cinema* con *la sua amica* Maria. Il film *comincia* alle venti. Paolo porta una camicia bianca e una cravatta rossa. Maria porta la sua camicetta gialla con i calzini gialli e una nuova gonna verde. Tutti e due portano le scarpe nere. Sono adesso le sette e un quarto e Paolo va *da* Maria.

al cinema	to the movie theater
la sua amica	his friend
comincia	starts
da	to the house of

1. Chi è l'amica di Paolo?
   A. sua madre
   B. Roberto
   C. sua sorella
   D. Maria

2. Dove vanno Paolo e Maria?
   A. in campagna
   B. al ristorante
   C. al cinema
   D. al parco

3. Di che colore è la cravatta di Paolo?
   A. verde
   B. rossa
   C. blu
   D. bianca

4. Di che colore sono i calzini di Maria?
   A. gialli
   B. marrone
   C. neri
   D. grigi

5. A che ora va Paolo alla casa di Maria?
   A. alle 7:15
   B. alle 6:45
   C. alle 6:30
   D. alle 8:00

6. A che ora comincia il film?
   A. alle sette
   B. alle sette e un quarto
   C. alle otto
   D. alle otto e mezzo

G Metti un pò di colore sull'orologio. *(Color the clock according to the directions.)*

Sono le nove.

1. il naso giallo
2. gli occhi azzurri
3. i capelli verdi
4. la faccia arancione
5. la bocca marrone
6. i piedi grigi

7. il numero quattro nero
8. il numero sei viola
9. il numero tre rosso
10. la lettera *s* bianca
11. la lettera *o* rosa
12. la lettera *n* nera

H Parliamo! You want to know at what time certain things take place, i.e. *la classe di matematica, il concerto, il picnic.* Start with, *A che ora _____?* Your partner should answer you by mentioning a specific time of the day or evening.

I I saluti. Your speaking partner will give you six times of day in Italian. For each, answer with the correct greeting: *Buongiorno, Buonasera,* or *Buonanotte.* When you finish, trade roles.

J Tocca a te! One of your classmates acts as quizmaster and the other classmates will answer. Walk around your room and point to an object. Ask, *Di che colore è _____?* Your classmate will answer, *È _____,* naming the correct color. If someone answers incorrectly, he/she drops out of the contest. Keep going, pointing to different objects, until you have just one classmate left. That person is the winner. The quizmaster determines if answers are correct.

Lingua viva!

Numero Verde Gratuito

800-929291

Mercoledì

RAIUNO
© 199/123000

6.10 È PROIBITO BALLARE - Telefilm
6.30 TG1
6.45 UNOMATTINA ESTATE - Contenitore
Con Stefano Ziantoni, Eleonora Daniele
All'interno: **TG1** (Edizioni alle ore 7.00 -
7.30 - 8.00 - 9.00 - 9.30)
9.45 TG PARLAMENTO
9.50 LA SIGNORA DEL WEST - Telefilm
10.35 UN CICLONE IN CONVENTO - Telefilm
Con Jutta Speidel, Fritz Wepper
11.25 APPUNTAMENTO AL CINEMA
11.30 TG1 - CHE TEMPO FA
11.40 UN MEDICO IN FAMIGLIA - Fiction
Con Lino Banfi, Giulio Scarpati, Claudia
Pandolfi, Milena Vukotic (Replica)
13.30 TELEGIORNALE
14.00 TG1 ECONOMIA - Rubrica
14.10 SOTTOCASA - Soap opera
Con Daniela Giordano, Giovanni Guidelli
14.35 LE SORELLE McLEOD - Telefilm
15.20 ATTRAZIONE PROIBITA
Film drammatico ●● (USA, 1997). Con
Cassidy Rae, Vincent Irizarry, Jamie Rose
Regia di Marina Sargenti
16.50 TG PARLAMENTO
16.55 CHE TEMPO FA - TG1
17.10 DON MATTEO 2 - Telefilm (Replica)
18.10 LA SIGNORA IN GIALLO - Telefilm
19.05 IL COMMISSARIO REX - Telefilm
Con Tobias Moretti
20.00 TELEGIORNALE
20.30 COTTI E MANGIATI - Sitcom
Con Flavio Insinna, Marina Massironi
21.00 UNA VOCE PER PADRE PIO
Conduce Massimo Giletti con la
partecipazione di Tosca D'Aquino
23.15 TG1 - Notiziario
23.20 20° SECOLO - TESTIMONI E
PROTAGONISTI - Documenti
0.20 TG1 - NOTTE - CHE TEMPO FA
0.50 APPUNTAMENTO AL CINEMA
0.55 SOTTOVOCE - Rubrica
Conduce Gigi Marzullo
1.25 RAI EDUCATIONAL

MAGHETTO AL NERO

LA PORTA
DI TOLOMEO

(6) Rosso ciliegia,
n tessuto tecnico
antivento,
con cappuccio.
Di PZeroPirelli
(460 €).

K **Look at the clippings and answer the following questions.**

1. Look at the watch then write the time in Italian. _____

2. Maghetto is a small wizard; what color is he? Write the answer in Italian and English.

   _____

3. What is the color of the 800 phone number? Write the answer in Italian and English.

   _____

4. What item in the clippings is *Rosso ciliegia?* _____

5. What is the color of the pan hanging on the wall? Write the answer in Italian and English.

   _____

L **Look at the clippings and answer the following questions.**

1. At what time can you watch "Dr. Quinn Medicine Woman," called in Italian "The Lady of the West"? _____

2. At what time can you watch a show about sisters? _____

3. At 6:10 PM, you can watch a show about a lady dressed in a specific color. Which color?

   _____

4. *Che tempo fa* is the weather forecast. How many times can you find out about the weather during the day? At what times? _____

5. *Telegiornale* means newscast. What are the times of the two newscasts of the day?

   _____

Proverbio

"Meglio tardi che mai. Better late than never."

Symtalk

M Scrivi nello spazio la parola giusta in italiano *(In the space, write the correct word in Italian.)*

1. _____ 2. _____ 3. _____ 4. _____ 5. _____

N Dì le frasi, poi scrivile in italiano. *(Say the sentences, then write them in Italian.)*

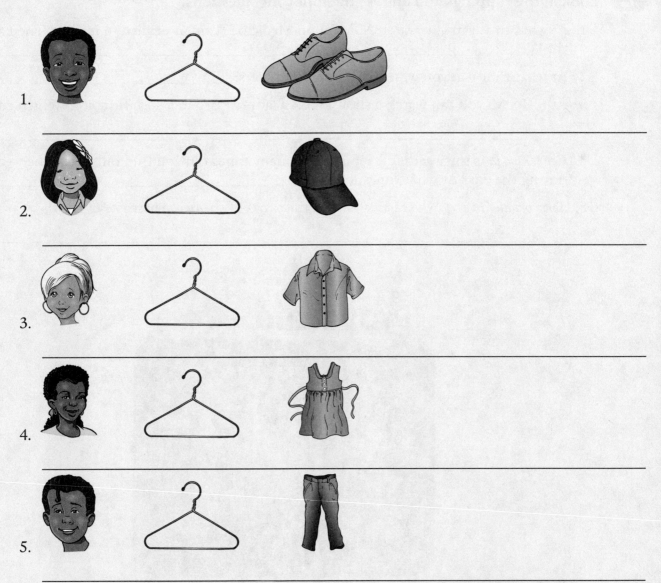

1. _____

2. _____

3. _____

4. _____

5. _____

O **Fate le domande e rispondete. Poi, scrivete il dialogo.** *(With a partner, ask the question or give the answer. Then, write the dialogue.)*

1.

_____

No, _____

_____

2.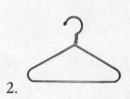

_____

No, _____

3.
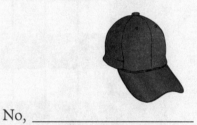

_____

No, _____

4.

_____

No, _____

_____

Il cruciverba

Orizzontale

4. Sono le due e un ____. (2:15)
6. ____ le nove. (9:00)
8. Sono le dieci ____ cinque. (9:55)
9. il colore del cioccolato
10. il colore del latte
12. il colore degli spinaci

Verticale

1. il colore di un'arancia
2. il colore del burro
3. il colore di una fragola
5. Che ____ sono?
7. È l'____. (1:00)
8. È mezzogiorno e ____. (12:30)
11. A ____ ora è il picnic?

Unit 14

La musica

Music

Tre grandi musicisti
(Three Great Musicians)

Antonio Vivaldi
1678–1741

Antonio Vivaldi (1678–1741) began his musical studies under the guidance of his father, a professional violinist. A Venetian by birth, young Antonio grew up to become a popular and successful baroque musician and composer. He was a violin teacher and director of a girls' school in his hometown. Although he also was an ordained Roman Catholic priest, Vivaldi put aside his religious interests in order to promote his musical career.

Baroque music emphasizes, among other things, vocal music such as the oratorio and the cantata, string instruments such as the harpsichord and the violin, and frequent use of major and minor keys. As a representative of the baroque period, Vivaldi was interested in both vocal and instrumental music. He was a contemporary of two other baroque composers, Antonio Soler of Spain and Johann Sebastian Bach of Germany.

Vivaldi wrote music for operas and church services, and songs for his favorite singing pupils. He is known best for developing the *Concerto Grosso,* an orchestral piece designed specifically for one or two instruments. He composed more than 500 concertos, including: *The Four Seasons* (Le Quattro stagioni), in four movements; *Concerto in C minor for Strings and Continuo;* and *Concerto in G major for Two Mandolins.* In spite of Vivaldi's talent for music and his great interest in earning money through it, he never learned to manage his money wisely. He died as a pauper at the age of 63.

Muzio Clementi (1752–1832) is one of Italy's outstanding representatives of the classical period of music. As a young boy he showed exceptional promise and quickly obtained the position of organist in his local church. At the age of 13, Muzio was discovered by a traveling Englishman. He left his place of birth, Rome, and journeyed to Dorset, England, where his benefactor gave him the opportunity to study music privately.

Muzio Clementi
1752–1832

At 22 Clementi moved to London and began to compose in the classical style of harmony and traditional structure. He created over 100 piano sonatas, and, in fact, is often referred to as the "Father of the Pianoforte." He wrote symphonies, conducted orchestras, taught piano students, and performed on the harpsichord. As a businessman, Clementi published the work of other composers (even those of Beethoven), and he directed the manufacturing of Clementi pianos. Finally, as an author, he published his own compositions as well as a textbook for piano students entitled *Introduction to the Art of Playing on the Pianoforte.*

Clementi traveled extensively throughout Europe, giving concert performances in Russia, Germany, France, and Italy. Although he never moved back to his native country, Clementi is still considered one of the great Italian composers of classical instrumental music.

Giuseppe Verdi (1813–1901) was born in the small village of Roncale where his parents owned an inn. His talent was recognized early, and at three, he was given a spinet (an instrument similar to the harpsichord). Verdi completed his classical-humanistic education and formal music training in Busseto and eventually became the town's official musician. Happiness, however, came neither easily nor quickly. He experienced several professional disappointments followed by the deaths of his wife and son.

Giuseppe Verdi
1813–1901

The composer's marches, songs, and church music brought him into the public eye, but it was his opera, *Nabucco*, which brought him instant recognition and popularity. Encouraged by the world-wide success of *Nabucco*, Verdi concentrated on producing operas. He chose stories or plays that he admired and that could be adapted into operatic forms. His choices now have become classics in the world of music such as *Aida, Falstaff, Otello, Rigoletto*, and *La Traviata*. He greatly admired the plays of Schiller, adapting *Kabal und Liebe* into *Luisa Millar, Die Rauber* into *I masnadieri*, and *Don Carlos* into the opera of the same name.

As a Romantic artist, Verdi wanted to express human emotions, reveal social injustice, and promote freedom. As a Romantic musician, he emphasized these themes through full orchestration and magnificent arias and duets. At his death, Verdi received national acclaim; the entire nation mourned the loss of its patriotic and popular native son.

Contemporary Musicians

Adriano Celentano is an Italian singer, songwriter, comedian, actor, and TV host. In addition, he is known as one of the most famous dancers of the Hula hoop craze. Celentano was very much influenced by Elvis Presley and has been a popular entertainer in Italy since the 1960s. His 1960 song "Azzurro" regained popularity in 2006 due to its use as the anthem of the Italian national football (soccer) team—the Azzurri—who won the FIFA World Cup that year.

Adriano Celentano

Laura Pausini is an Italian pop singer who is also very popular in Spain and Latin America. She has recorded albums in Spanish, Portuguese, and English. She recorded her first album at age 13. Pausini is well known for her soulful voice, love songs, and romantic ballads. She has sold over 26 million records worldwide and became the first Italian female to win a Grammy Award.

Andrea Bocelli is both an operatic tenor and a classical crossover singer. To date, he has recorded four complete operas—*La Bohème, Il Trovatore, Werther,* and *Tosca*—in addition to various classical and pop albums. At age 12, Bocelli won his first music competition. That same year, Bocelli was struck blind as a result of glaucoma and an accident while playing soccer. After working for one year as a lawyer, he took singing lessons from Italian maestro Luciano Bettarini and pursued a full-time music career.

Laura Pausini

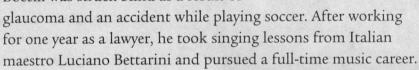

Andrea Bocelli

Before becoming a successful singer, **Luciano Ligabue** held various jobs in agriculture and in factories. Ligabue has gained fame as one of the most successful Italian rock stars, finding fans mainly among younger audiences. In addition to success in music, he has directed films, published short stories and poetry, and raised money for political and social causes.

Luciano Ligabue

Le attività

A Quale compositore appartiene a questo periodo? *(Give the full name of the composer whose music is called.)*

   1. baroque

_____

   2. classical

_____

   3. romantic

_____

B Fai corrispondere gli oggetti del gruppo *A* con quelli del gruppo *B*.

A	B
1. _____ *Aida*	A. type of music made famous by Vivaldi
2. _____ *Concerto Grosso*	B. opera by Verdi
3. _____ *Introduction to the Art of Playing the Pianoforte*	C. work by Clementi
	D. work by Vivaldi
4. _____ *The Four Seasons*	E. book by Clementi
5. _____ piano sonatas	

C Indovina chi . . . *(Guess who . . .)*

   1. . . . had two completely different careers.

_____

   2. . . . combined plays and music.

_____

   3. . . . manufactured and published.

_____

   4. . . . became a national hero.

_____

   5. . . . played both the piano and the harpsichord.

_____

D **Completa le analogie.**

1. *Nabucco:* _____ = *Concerto in G major for Two Madolins:* Vivaldi

2. Roncale: Verdi = _____: Clementi

3. _____: Clementi = violin: Vivaldi

4. Vivaldi: concerto = Verdi: _____

5. _____: Clementi = Antonio: Vivaldi

E **Fai corrispondere il nome all' illustrazione.**

1. _____

2. _____

3. _____

F Decifra le parole. *(Unscramble the words.)*

1. ERPOA _____

2. OTCONCER _____

3. TAASON _____

4. ERDIV _____

5. TIMENELC _____

G Tocca a te! **Choose an Italian singer, musician, or composer. Find out as much as you can about the person's life and music. Report your findings to the class. A musical excerpt on an audio CD would add a nice touch to your presentation. Luciano Pavarotti, Giovanni Pierluigi da Palestrina, Andrea Bocelli, Eros Ramazzotti, Zucchero, and Vasco Rossi are a few.**

Proverbio

" Cambiano i suonatori ma la musica è sempre quella.

The melody's changed but the song remains the same. "

dal **rock** *allo* swing

A marzo quattro appuntamenti da non perdere all'Auditorium Parco della Musica

Scegli la tua canzone preferita
e trasformala nella suoneria del tuo telefonino!
Invia un SMS con il codice della canzone al 48467
e la riceverai subito sul cellulare!

Per clienti Tim, Vodafone e Wind

Esempio:
Per ricevere la suoneria di "Andavo a cento all'ora", invia un SMS con scritto **13483** al numero **48467**

13483

I Favolosi anni '60

Andavo a cento all'ora	13483
Tu vuo fa' l'americano	13484
Fatti mandare dalla mamma	13485
Viva la pappa col pomodoro	13486
Quando quando quando	13487
Caravan Petrol	13488
La bambola	13489
L'esercito del surf	13490
Il mondo	13491
Senza fine	13492

Per controllare se il tuo telefonino è compatibile e per verificare i costi del servizio, vai all'ultima pagina

Calendario

CHISCIOTTE E GLI INVINCIBILI
di Erri De Luca
con Erri De Luca, Gianmaria
Testa e Gabriele Mirabassi
15 e 16 marzo 2006 ore 21.00
Sala Petrassi

SIMPLE MINDS
in tour
19 marzo 2006 ore 21.00
Sala Santa Cecilia

GIANNA NANNINI
"Grazie"
23 marzo 2006 ore 21.00
Sala Sinopoli

THE WORLD FAMOUS
COUNT BASIE ORCHESTRA
Dir. by Bill Hughes
feat. Butch Miles
29 marzo 2006 ore 21.00
Sala Santa Cecilia

Info: tel. **06 80241281**
www.auditorium.com

Stregato dalla danza
Musica
PER GLI OCCHI

H Look at the clippings and answer the following questions.

1. In one clipping, music is paired with a body part. Which part is it? Write the word in English and in Italian.

   _____

2. What does *Calendario* mean in English?

   _____

3. At what time does the concert of the *Chisciotte e gli Invincibili* start?

   _____

4. *Gianna Nannini* is a famous Italian singer, what is the title of her concert?

   _____

5. What does the title mean in English?

   _____

I Look at the big yellow and red clipping in the middle of the page and answer the following questions.

1. The first line says "Choose your preferred song." What is the Italian word that means "song"?

   _____

2. *Telefono* means phone, what do you think *telefonino* means?

   _____

3. Can you guess what *cellulare* means?

   _____

4. What do you think the word *esempio* means?

   _____

5. This is a list of songs from the *favolosi anni 60*. What do you think that means in English?

   _____

Symtalk

J Scrivi nello spazio la parola giusta in italiano. *(In the space, write the correct word in Italian.)*

1. _____
   _____

2. _____

3. _____

4. _____

K Dì le frasi, poi scrivile in italiano. *(Say the sentences then write them in Italian.)*

1.

   _____

2.

   _____

3.

   _____

4.

   _____

5.

_____

L Fate le domande e rispondete. Poi, scrivete il dialogo. *(With a partner, ask the question or give the answer. Then, write the dialogue.)*

1.

_____   _____

2.

_____   _____

3.

_____   _____

4.

_____   _____

Il cruciverba

Orizzontale

5. name of Vivaldi's musical period
6. Clementi was the "Father of the ____"
9. kind of stage production
11. Country where Clementi composed
13. Clementi is a representative of this musical age
14. Verdi's first instrument
15. initials of the Baroque composer

Verticale

1. Verdi's first name
2. Verdi's opera which brought him fame and popularity
3. over 100 of these were composed by Clementi
4. *The ____ Seasons*
7. Clementi's first musical job
8. opera by Verdi: *La ____*
10. Vivaldi's first career choice
12. ____ *Carlos*

Unit 15

Il tempo e le stagioni
Weather and Seasons

Il vocabolario

Che tempo fa?   How's the weather?

Fa bel tempo.

Cosi' cosi.

C'è il sole.
It's sunny.

Fa caldo.
It's hot.

Fa fresco.
It's cool.

Tira vento./
È ventoso.
It's windy.

È afoso.
It's humid.

È nuvoloso./
È coperto.
It's cloudy.

Fa brutto tempo.

Tuona.
It's thundering.

Piove.
It's raining.

Lampeggia.
It's lightning.

Fa freddo.
It's cold.

Nevica.
It's snowing.

Quale stagione è?
What's the season?
È …
It's …

Le quattro stagioni

l'estate

la primavera

l'inverno

l'autunno

- in estate/d'estate = *in the summer (etc.)*
- Notice the noun forms of some verbs:

il tuono	=	thunder	→	**Tuona.**	=	It's thundering.
il fulmine/lampo	=	lightning	→	**Lampeggia.**	=	It's lightning.
la pioggia	=	rain	→	**Piove.**	=	It's raining.
la neve	=	snow	→	**Nevica.**	=	It's snowing.

MADRE: **Porta il tuo ombrello.**
FIGLIO: **Perchè?**
MADRE: **Perchè piove.**

MADRE: **Porta i tuoi occhiali da sole.**
FIGLIO: **Perchè?**
MADRE: **Perchè c'è il sole.**

PADRE: **Porta il tuo cappello.**
FIGLIA: **Perchè?**
PADRE: **Perchè fa freddo.**

portare = to wear (also, take along)

Le attività

Quale immagine va con ogni frase? *(Match each picture with a sentence.)*

A		B

1. _____E_____

A. C'è il sole.

2. _____D_____

B. Lampeggia.

3. _____A_____

C. Piove.

4. _____C_____

D. Tira vento.

5. _____B_____

E. Fa freddo.

Che tempo fa? Rispondi in italiano. *(How's the weather? Answer this question in Italian according to each picture.)*

1. _il piove_

2. _____

3. _tira vento_

4. _Fa freddo_

5. _C'è il sole_

A   B

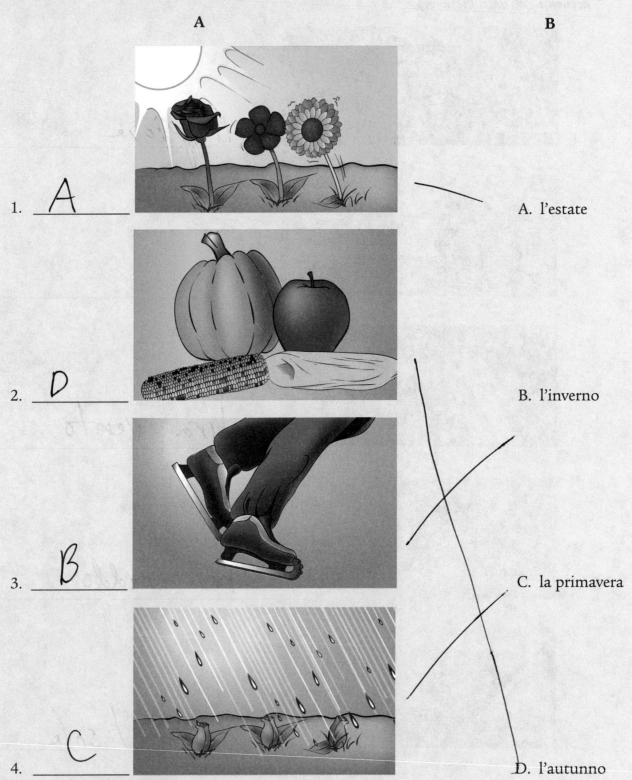

1. _____A_____   A. l'estate

2. _____D_____   B. l'inverno

3. _____B_____   C. la primavera

4. _____C_____   D. l'autunno

D *Un pò di pratica.* Write in <u>Column 1</u> the English meaning of each Italian word. When you have finished the entire column, cover the column of Italian words at the left. Then in <u>Column 2</u>, change the English words into Italian.

	Column 1 (English)	**Column 2** (Italian)
1. il sole	_____	_____
2. il fulmine	_____	_____
3. la primavera	_____	_____
4. l'estate	_____	_____
5. il tempo	_____	_____
6. l'autunno	_____	_____
7. la stagione	_____	_____
8. fresco	_____	_____
9. caldo	_____	_____
10. piove	_____	_____
11. l'inverno	_____	_____
12. brutto (tempo)	_____	_____
13. il tuono	_____	_____
14. freddo	_____	_____

E **Metti insieme A e B.** *(Match column A with column B.)*

A	**B**
1. _E_ la pioggia	A. C'è il sole.
2. _D_ la neve	B. Tuona.
3. _B_ il tuono	C. Lampeggia.
4. _C_ il fulmine	D. Nevica.
5. _A_ il sole	E. Piove.

F *Che tempo fa?* Use the cues to write statements in Italian about the weather.

1. mittens and parka

_____

2. sunglasses

_____

3. lightning bolts

_____

4. light sweater

_____

5. outdoor tennis court

_____

6. umbrella

_____

7. snowflakes

_____

8. air conditioner

_____

9. sailboat

_____

10. rain, wind, and hail

_____

G **Leggi il brano e completa le frasi.** *(Read the passage and then, complete the following sentences.)*

> ### Le quattro stagioni
>
> In inverno, fa molto freddo. Nevica molto. La neve è bianca. In primavera, fa fresco e piove molto. Fa caldo e c'è molto sole in estate. In autunno, tira vento e fa fresco di nuovo. Le quattro stagioni sono molto interessanti.

di nuovo	again
molto	very

1. In inverno __C__.
   A. è afoso
   B. tuona
   C. fa freddo
   D. fa caldo

2. Piove molto __A__.
   A. in primavera
   B. in estate
   C. in inverno
   D. in autunno

3. Fa molto caldo _____.
   A. in inverno
   B. in autunno
   C. in primavera
   D. in estate

4. Ci sono _____ stagioni.
   A. cinque
   B. quattro
   C. sei
   D. tre

H **Parliamo!** Think of three clothing items or accessories. For each one you select, ask your partner to say how the weather is. Then reverse the roles. He/she will suggest to you three new cues and you should answer.

> **Modello:** **A:** gli occhiali da sole
> Che tempo fa?
> **B:** C'è il sole.

I **Tocca a te!** Select five cities in various parts of the world and five different months. Use cities in different continents and hemispheres. Ask your partner about the weather in that city. Your partner then should respond appropriately according to the city and month. Don't forget that when it's summer in the northern hemisphere, it is winter in the southern hemisphere! Write your answers on a piece of paper.

> **Modello:** **A:** Che tempo fa a Tokyo a gennaio?
> **B:** Fa freddo.

Proverbio

66 È la gaia pioggerella a far crescer l'erba bella.

It's the merry drizzle that makes grass grow fine. 99

Lingua viva!

TUTTE LE RICETTE PER UN'ESTATE DIVERTENTE, FRESCA, CREATIVA.

LA CUCINA DELL'ESTATE:

1 Pasta	23 giugno	6 Verdure	28 luglio	
2 Pasta in insalata	30 giugno	7 Dolci	4 agosto	
3 Riso	7 luglio	8 Frutta	11 agosto	
4 Carne	14 luglio	9 Conserve	18 agosto	
5 Pesce	21 luglio	10 Picnic e buffet	25 agosto	

Ingredienti per 8 persone: ogni venerdì recatevi nella più vicina edicola. Scoprirete La cucina dell'estate, la nuova collana del Corriere della Sera dedicata alle ricette più creative e sfiziose. Dieci monografie inedite: dalla pasta al pesce alla griglia, dalla carne ai dolci di frutta, dalle conserve alle torte salate. Idee e consigli per tanti piatti appetitosi, leggeri e veloci da gustare in compagnia.

DA VENERDÌ 7 LUGLIO "RISO, ORZO, FARRO, COUSCOUS" A SOLI € 6,90.

CORRIERE DELLA SERA

CAPIRE IL DOMANI, OGNI GIORNO.

CITTA' ITALIANE

	min	max		min	max		min	max
						Bari	22	29
				14	24	Napoli	21	28
			Bologna	15	26	Potenza	19	26
	min	max	Firenze	15	26	S. M. Leuca	24	32
	13	26	Pisa	14	25	R. Calabria	24	30
Aosta	10	23	Ancona	15	25	Palermo	25	29
Bolzano	14	24	Perugia	16	27	Catania	20	31
Verona	17	24	Pescara	10	25	Messina	25	30
Trieste	15	24	L'Aquila	18	25	Alghero	19	29
Venezia	16	25	Roma Ciamp.	19	25	Cagliari	17	30
Milano	14	23	Roma Fium.	15	25			
Torino	12	21	Campobasso					
Cuneo	20	25						
Genova	16	24						
Imperia								

CITTA' ESTERE

	min	max			min	max	
				Lisbona	22	33	sereno
				Londra	16	24	variabile
	min	max		Los Angeles	19	29	sereno
	12	21	variabile	Madrid	13	28	sereno
Amsterdam	22	35	sereno	Montreal	15	25	variabile
Atene	25	24	variabile	Mosca	12	22	variabile
Bangkok	13	22	nuvoloso	New York	20	27	variabile
Berlino	12	33	sereno	Nizza	16	25	sereno
Bruxelles	14	29	variabile	Parigi	13	23	variabile
Bucarest	17	17	sereno	Pechino	23	31	variabile
Budapest	8	19	nuvoloso	Praga	16	23	pioggia
Buenos Aires	12	21	variabile	Rio de Janeiro	15	21	variabile
Copenaghen	16	25	nuvoloso	Sofia	15	33	sereno
Dublino	14	30	sereno	Sydney	11	17	variabile
Francoforte	19	19	variabile	Tokyo	24	34	pioggia
Gerusalemme	16	22	variabile	Varsavia	12	24	pioggia
Ginevra	12	19	variabile	Vienna	17	22	pioggia
Helsinki	7	34	sereno				
Johannesburg	23	29	variabile				
Il Cairo	23	29	variabile				
Istanbul							

arte a Bologna

CITTÀ D'ARTE

Primavera

Autunno.

OGGI. Sulle regioni di Nord Ovest, sulle regioni costiere tirreniche e sulle isole, sereno e poco nuvoloso. Sulle regioni di Nord Est e su quelle centro settentrionali adriatiche nuvolosità irregolare con possibilità di temporali pomeridiani sul Trentino Alto Adige e sulle zone appenniniche. Sereno o poco nuvoloso al Sud.

DOMANI. Al sereno del mattino farà riscontro, nel pomeriggio, lo sviluppo di nubi cumuliformi sui rilievi con possibilità di qualche temporale sul Friuli Venezia Giulia. Temperature ovunque in aumento di alcuni gradi.

J **Look at the clippings and answer the following questions.**

1. What does *autunno* mean in English?

   _____

2. The city of Bologna is hosting an Art Show. Can you tell in which season?

   _____

3. *Citta Italiane* means Italian cities, what do you think *Citta Estere* means?

   _____

4. Based on the temperature/weather chart, which Italian city is going to have the coldest weather today?

   _____

5. Which world city is going to have the warmest weather today?

   _____

K **Look at the clippings and answer the following questions.**

1. Find the Italian word for "today."

   _____

2. Find the Italian word for "tomorrow."

   _____

3. What is the weather in Bruxelles today? Write the answer in English and in Italian.

   _____

4. What is the weather in Praga today?

   _____

5. Write today's weather forecast for the following Italian cities.
   A. Milano _____
   B. Perugia _____
   C. Venezia _____

Symtalk

  Scrivi nello spazio la parola giusta in italiano. *(In the space, write the correct word in Italian.)*

1. _____   2. _____   3. _____   4. _____   5. _____

M Dì le frasi, poi scrivile in italiano. *(Say the sentences then write them in Italian.)*

1. _____

2. _____

3. _____

4. _____

5. _____

Fate le domande e rispondete. Poi, scrivete il dialogo. *(With a partner, ask the question or give the answer. Then, write the dialogue.)*

1.  **?**

_____   No, _____

2.  **?**

_____   No, _____

3.  **?**

_____   Sì, _____

4.  **?**

_____   No, _____

5.  **?**

_____   No, _____

Il cruciverba

Orizzontale

1. Autumn is a _____ of the year.
3. damp and clammy
6. slightly *freddo*
11. season when it's cold and snowy
13. when you need an umbrella
15. season of long school recess and family vacations
16. nature's rebirth

Verticale

1. source of light and heat
2. It's cloudy: È _____.
4. _____ *bel tempo.*
5. a flash of light in the sky
7. weather in the summer: *Fa* _____.
8. when you hear a loud noise in the sky
9. *Fa brutto* _____.
10. weather when you want to keep warm: *Fa* _____.
12. what the weather does when rain freezes
14. It's windy: *Tira* _____.

Unit 16

I giorni e i mesi
Days and Months

Il vocabolario

Che giorno è oggi? **Oggi è . . .**
What day is today?   Today is . . .

Monday lunedì	martedì	mercoledì	giovedì	venerdì	sabato	domenica
	1	2	3	4	5	6
7	8	9	10	11	12	13
14	15	16	17	18	19	20
21	22	23	24	25	26	27
28	29	30	31			

Quando è la festa?   When is the holiday?   **Il ventiquattro giugno**   June 24
È domani.   It's tomorrow.   **Il quindici settembre**   September 15
Qual'è la data di oggi? What is the date today? **Dal 4 al 29 (il ventinove aprile)** 4 - 29 (April 29)
È il primo maggio.   It's May first.

marzo aprile maggio

settembre ottobre novembre

giugno luglio agosto

dicembre gennaio febbraio

- When you say the first day of any month, use the word *primo*: *È il primo gennaio.*

- When you write the date, be sure to put the day before the month.

- Neither months nor days are capitalized in Italian.

Il quaderno di Natalia

Studia per l'esame d'inglese:

1. tomorrow
2. the day after tomorrow
3. yesterday
4. the day before yesterday
5. the day
6. the holiday
7. the school day
8. the birthday (domani)
9. the week
10. the weekend (Che fortuna, finalmente!)
11. the month
12. today

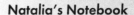

Natalia's Notebook

Study for the Italian test:

1. domani
2. dopodomani
3. ieri
4. l'altro ieri
5. il giorno
6. la festa
7. il giorno di scuola
8. il compleanno
9. la settimana
10. il fine settimana
11. il mese
12. oggi

ENRICO: **Quando è il tuo compleanno, Giorgio?**
When is your birthday, Giorgio?

GIORGIO: **È dopodomani, l'otto giugno.**
It's the day after tomorrow, on June eighth.

MARIO: **Quando è l'esame d'inglese?**
When is the English test?

MICHELE: **È martedì.**
It's on Tuesday.

CAROLINA: **Che cos' hai oggi, Andrea?**
What do you have today, Andrew?

ANDREA: **Niente! Oggi ho il giorno libero.**
Nothing! Today I've got a free day.

ANNA: **Che cos' hai mercoledì?**
What do you have on Wednesday?

GINA: **Ho la mia lezione di pianoforte.**
I have my piano lesson.

...edi	martedì	merc...
	1	2
7	8	9
	15	

Weekdays and Mythology

Derivations and Comparisons

I giorni	Roman Mythology
lunedì	day honoring the moon god (*luna*, Latin name for moon)
martedì	day honoring Mars, the god of war
mercoledì	day honoring Mercury, messenger of the gods
giovedì	day honoring Jupiter or Jove, father of all the gods
venerdì	day honoring Venus, goddess of love
sabato	day honoring Saturn, god of the harvest and agriculture
domenica	day honoring the Lord (*dominus*, Latin name for the Lord) Christian conversion of *dies solis*, day of the sun (Sunday) or day honoring the god of the sun

Le attività

 A **Scrivi la data in numeri.** *(Write in numerical form the dates that your teacher reads.)*

> **Modello:** Teacher says: December 30
> You write: 30/12

1. _____

2. _____

3. _____

4. _____

5. _____

B **Questo mese.** *(Label the current month. Include the names of the days and all the numbers.)*

C Scrivi le date. *(Write the dates.)*

> **Modello:** Tuesday, February 11th
> martedì, l'undici febbraio

1. Wednesday, October 22nd

   _____

2. Sunday, August 13th

   _____

3. Thursday, May 1st

   _____

4. Saturday, January 31st

   _____

5. Friday, April 26th

   _____

D Rispondi in inglese. *(Answer the following questions in English.)*

1. If the date is 12/3, what is the month and what is the day?

   _____

2. Which part of the solar system is associated with the name *dies solis*?

   _____

3. Which Roman god was a fast runner?

   _____

E Scegli la risposta corretta. *(Choose the correct answers.)*

1. Quale giorno è oggi?
   A. la settimana
   B. lunedì
   C. luglio
   D. mese

2. Qual'è la data di oggi?
   A. Oggi è una festa.
   B. Oggi, non ho niente.
   C. Oggi è il dieci gennaio.
   D. Oggi è domenica.

Rileggi i dialoghi dell'unità, poi rispondi alle domande. *(The following questions are based on the dialogues presented in this unit. Review them before you choose your answers.)*

3. Che cos'ha Giorgio l'otto giugno?
   A. il fine settimana
   B. marzo
   C. il compleanno
   D. martedì

4. Che cos' ha Michele martedì?
   A. Ha due cani e un gatto.
   B. Ha un esame d'inglese.
   C. Ha una casa a San Gimignano.
   D. Ha una piccola famiglia.

5. Quando ha la lezione di pianoforte Gina?
   A. mercoledì
   B. martedì
   C. venerdì
   D. lunedì

6. Chi ha un giorno libero oggi?
   A. Enrico
   B. Gina
   C. Carolina
   D. Andrea

F Trova la parola italiana per ogni parola inglese. *(Match the Italian with the English.)*

1. _____ oggi
2. _____ dopodomani
3. _____ l'altro ieri
4. _____ domani
5. _____ ieri

A. yesterday
B. day after tomorrow
C. today
D. tomorrow
E. day before yesterday

G Scrivi in italiano. *(Write in Italian.)*

1. the third month of the year _____

2. the day that honors the Roman father of all the gods _____

3. the day that honors the Roman goddess, Venus _____

4. this month's showers bring May flowers _____

5. the first day of the Italian week _____

6. the month of the national holiday in the United States _____

7. the month in which Halloween is celebrated _____

8. the month of your *compleanno* _____

Identifica il giorno della settimana. *(In Italian, identify the weekday according to the illustration.)*

1. _____

2. _____

3. _____

4. _____

5. _____

6. _____

7. _____

I **Leggi il brano e scegli le risposte corrette. (*Read the passage and then select the correct answers.*)**

Oggi è un giorno speciale per Luca, un ragazzo italiano. Luca è andato a trovare il suo amico Gregorio che abita in Germania. È domenica, nove luglio. È estate e fa bel tempo. È anche il giorno della partita finale del *campionato di calcio più importante del mondo*. È *il campionato mondiale*. L'Italia *gioca* contro la Francia. Le due *squadre* giocano a Berlino. Generalmente, *i biglietti* sono difficili da trovare, *ma* Luca e Gregorio hanno i biglietti. Luca è molto allegro oggi.

il campionato di calcio	soccer championship	**le squadre**	teams
più importante del mondo	most important in the world	**i biglietti**	tickets
gioca	is playing	**ma**	but
il campionato mondiale	the World Cup		

1. Che giorno è oggi?
   A. lunedì
   B. venerdì
   C. martedì
   D. domenica *(circled)*

2. Qual'è la data?
   A. il nove luglio *(circled)*
   B. l'undici luglio
   C. il dieci novembre
   D. l'undici novembre

3. È un giorno speciale per Luca?
   A. Sì, molto. *(circled)*
   B. No.
   C. Abbastanza.
   D. È il suo compleanno.

4. Chi è Gregorio?
   A. il fratello di Luca
   B. lo zio di Luca
   C. l'insegnante di Luca
   D. l'amico di Luca *(circled)*

5. Quale squadra gioca contro la Francia?
   A. La Spagna
   B. La Germania
   C. L'Italia *(circled)*
   D. Berlino

6. Come si sente oggi Luca?
   A. allegro *(circled)*
   B. triste
   C. fresco
   D. interessante

J **Parliamo!** **Find out the day your partner has each of these: his/her birthday** *(il compleanno)*, **a music lesson** *(una lezione di musica)*, **a big test** *(un esame)*. **Start with** *Che giorno è oggi?* **He/she should answer by saying a specific day of the week. Then he/she will ask you when three other things are:** *la festa, il compleanno di Natalia* **and** *il pranzo sull'erba.* **He/she should start with** *Quando è _____?* **You should answer with a general time such as today, tomorrow, or the day after tomorrow.**

K **Tocca a te!** **Find out whether you and your classmate know your days. You start by saying,** *Oggi è lunedì.* **Your classmate says,** *Domani è martedì.* **You finish by saying** *Dopodomani è mercoledì.* **Then your partner goes back to:** *Oggi è _____,* **etc. Continue until you both have identified all the weekdays.**

Proverbio

> " Trenta giorni ha novembre,
> con april, giugno e settembre,
> di ventotto ce n' è uno,
> tutti gli altri ne han trentuno.
>
> Thirty days has November,
> with April, June and September,
> with 28 there is only one,
> all the rest have 31. "

Lingua viva!

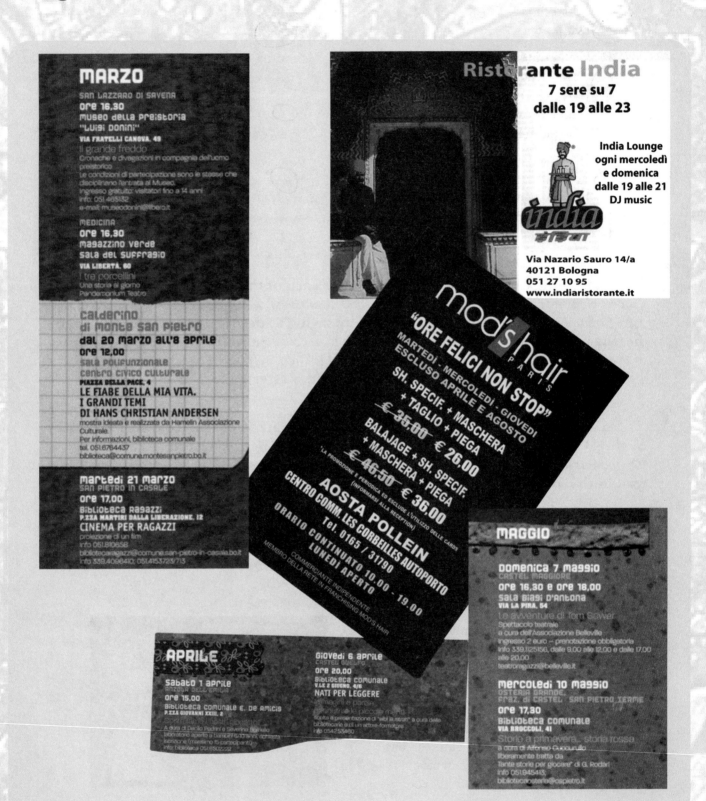

MARZO

SAN LAZZARO DI SAVENA
ORE 16,30
MUSEO DELLA PREISTORIA
"LUIGI DONINI"
VIA FRATELLI CANOVA, 49
Il grande freddo
Cronache e divagazioni in compagnia dell'uomo
preistorico
Le condizioni di partecipazione sono le stesse che
disciplinano l'entrata al Museo.
Ingresso gratuito: visitatori fino a 14 anni
Info: 051 465332
e-mail museodonini@libero.it

MEDICINA
ORE 16,30
MAGAZZINO VERDE
SALA DEL SUFFRAGIO
VIA LIBERTÀ, 60
I tre porcellini
Una storia al giorno
Pandemonium Teatro

Calderino
di Monte San Pietro
DAL 20 MARZO ALL'8 APRILE
ORE 12,00
SALA POLIFUNZIONALE
CENTRO CIVICO CULTURALE
PIAZZA DELLA PACE, 4
LE FIABE DELLA MIA VITA.
I GRANDI TEMI
DI HANS CHRISTIAN ANDERSEN
mostra ideata e realizzata da Hamelin Associazione
Culturale.
Per informazioni, biblioteca comunale
tel. 051.6764437
biblioteca@comune.montesanpietro.bo.it

MARTEDÌ 21 MARZO
SAN PIETRO IN CASALE
ORE 17,00
BIBLIOTECA RAGAZZI
P.ZZA MARTIRI DELLA LIBERAZIONE, 12
CINEMA PER RAGAZZI
proiezione di un film
Info 051.817658
bibliotecaragazzi@comune.san-pietro-in-casale.bo.it
Info 339.4098410; 051.4153723/713

MAGGIO

DOMENICA 7 MAGGIO
CASTEL MAGGIORE
ORE 16,30 E ORE 18,00
SALA BIAGI D'ANTONA
VIA LA PIRA, 54
Le avventure di Tom Sawyer
Spettacolo teatrale
a cura dell'Associazione Belleville
Ingresso 2 euro – prenotazione obbligatoria
Info 339.1125156, dalle 9.00 alle 12.00 e dalle 17.00
alle 20.00
teatroragazzi@belleville.it

MERCOLEDÌ 10 MAGGIO
OSTERIA GRANDE,
FRAZ. DI CASTEL SAN PIETRO TERME
ORE 17,30
BIBLIOTECA COMUNALE
VIA BROCCOLI, 41
Storie a primavera... storia rossa
a cura di Alfonso Cuccurullo
liberamente tratta da
Tante storie per giocare di G. Rodari
Info 051.945413;
bibliotecaosteria@ospietro.it

APRILE

SABATO 1 APRILE
ANZOLA DELL'EMILIA
ORE 15,00
BIBLIOTECA COMUNALE E. DE AMICIS
P.ZZA GIOVANNI XXIII, 2
A cura di Cecilia Padrini e Severino Borrello
laboratorio aperto a bambini 6/10 anni, richiesta
iscrizione (massimo 15 partecipanti)
Info: biblioteca 051.6502222

GIOVEDÌ 6 APRILE
CASTEL GUELFO
ORE 20,00
BIBLIOTECA COMUNALE
V.LE 2 GIUGNO, 4/6
NATI PER LEGGERE
immagini e parole
per nutrire le piccole menti
scelta a presentazione di "albi illustrati" a cura della
bibliotecaria ed è un attore-formatore
Info 0542.53460

L These are fun activities organized by various libraries for young readers. Look at the clippings and answer the following questions.

1. Name the three months represented in the clippings. Write the answer in English and in Italian.

   _____

2. What day of the week is May 7th?

   _____ Domenica _____

3. What show can the children see on May 7th?

   _____ Le avventure di Tom Sawyer _____

4. *Nati per leggere* means "born to read." What day, what month, and at what time is this activity offered?

   _____ Giovedì 6 Aprile _____

5. What day of the week is April Fool's Day?

   _____ Sabato _____

M Look at the clippings and answer the following questions.

1. What days of the week can you get your hair done in this salon?

   _____ Martedì-Mercoledì-Giovedì _____

2. *Escluso* means "excluded." Which two months have a different schedule?

   _____ Aprile e Agosto _____

3. At what time can you eat at this Indian restaurant?

   _____

4. At the Indian restaurant, you can listen to some music two days a week. Which days?

   _____

Symtalk

N Scrivi nello spazio la parola giusta in italiano. *(In the space, write the corret word in Italian.)*

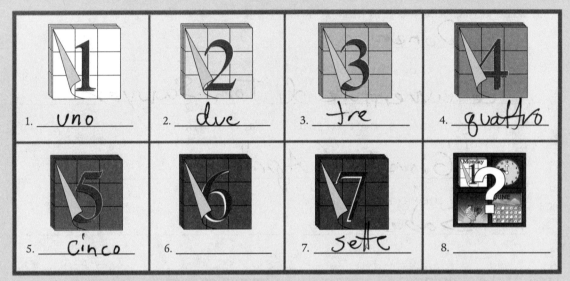

1. _uno_
2. _due_
3. _tre_
4. _quattro_
5. _cinco_
6. _____
7. _sette_
8. _____

O Dì le frasi, poi scrivile in italiano. *(Say the sentences, then write them in Italian.)*

1.

_____

2.

_____

3.

_____

4.

_____

P Fate le domande e rispondete. Poi, scrivete il dialogo. *(With a partner, ask the question or give the answer. Then, write the dialogue.)*

1.

_____

2.

_____

3.

_____

4.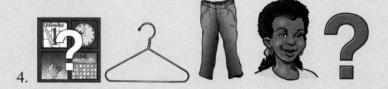

_____

5.

_____

Il cruciverba

Orizzontale

2. Saturn's day
4. day named for the Roman goddess of love
5. seven of these make a week
6. day of the moon or Moon-Day
9. There are twelve of these in a year.
10. last full month of winter
12. autumn month of thirty days
14. month that brings flowers
15. tenth month
16. yesterday's tomorrow

Verticale

1. month in which summer ends and autumn begins
3. first full month of spring
7. month in which spring ends and summer begins
8. last month of the year
11. month named for Julius Caesar
13. month named for the Roman god of war

Unit 17

La letteratura

Literature

Tre autori meravigliosi (Three Great Authors)

Dante Alighieri
1265–1320

Italy's greatest poet is **Dante Alighieri** (1265–1320), a man who has had a remarkable influence on the literature of the western world. Born in the city-state of Florence, Dante (as he is generally called today), enjoyed a good education and the advantages of a middle-class upbringing. His political career, however, eventually clashed with the religious factions of the time. Dante was sent into exile for many years. During his travels around Northern Italy, he learned much about people and politics. Because of his political and religious opinions, he was not allowed to return to Florence. He died in the city of Ravenna.

Dante's literary works touch upon a wide range of subjects and show his knowledge of philosophy, art, music, and ancient cultures. An early work, *La Vita Nuova,* is a collection of poems dedicated to the memory of Beatrice, a woman who was destined to marry another man. These poems are lyrical; they express his feelings of love and admiration as well as those of loss and resignation. Another work, *De Vulgari Eloquentia,* is written in Latin. It concerns the family of European languages, and describes the special relationship between Latin and the newly evolving Italian.

The poet's most famous work is entitled *La Divina Commedia (The Divine Comedy).* In the form of a long narrative poem, it is actually a critical evaluation of the people around him and their systems of justice. In this work, Dante describes a journey through hell and purgatory to heaven. Along the way, he surprised readers by placing some socially prominent "good" people in hell, and showing some people whom society had judged to be "bad" in heaven. The poem shows Dante's version of justice.

Literary critics and readers alike agree that Dante's lyric poetry is magnificent. The author excels in giving colorful and imaginative descriptions of realistic and ethical situations. Dante brings words to life, seemingly without effort, but he carefully plans every ode and every stanza. In his (now) famous letter to the Lord of Verona, Dante writes that poetry is 10 percent inspiration and 90 percent perspiration.

La letteratura

As a small boy in Venice, **Carlo Goldoni** (1707–1793) was very interested in the theater. Like young Schiller in Germany, Goldoni studied medicine and law, but he was never able to resist his attraction to the stage. He gave up a law practice in Padova to devote his career to the dramatic arts.

Goldoni was displeased by the prevalent style of drama called *commedia dell' arte.* According to this style, characters in a play were supposed to be just like the masks they wore: obvious and straightforward. Goldoni found that such characters seemed lifeless and dull. He wanted to reform this practice by bringing life and personality into a stage character. He believed that all drama, comedies and tragedies, should have strong character development. He wrote over 260 works for the stage. In all of his works, he showed realistic characters with strengths, weaknesses, moods, tempers, and consciences.

Carlo Goldoni

1707–1793

Goldoni earned the nickname "Father of the Italian Comedy." He was a master at blending funny and serious themes and combining humor with ethical judgments. Three of his most famous plays are *La Bottega del caffè (The Coffee House), Il Bugiardo (The Liar),* and *I Rusteghi (The Rustics).*

Because of some unpleasant rivalry with other Italian playwrights, Goldoni went to France. In Paris, he became the director of the Italian Theater, but he was soon disappointed. The job did not require his innovative skills and no one appreciated his talent and ideas. Goldoni soon left this post to become an Italian tutor for the French royal family. When the Revolutionaries took control of the government, he lost his money and any hope for a secure and peaceful retirement. He died in Versailles, France.

Alessandro Manzoni

1785–1873

Alessandro Manzoni (1785–1873) is considered by many people to be the greatest Italian novelist. He was born and raised in Milano and lived for a time in France before returning to Italy.

His literary works reflect the religious values and the ideals that he cherished throughout his life. These were, among others, patriotism and compassion. As for the political controversy, whether to maintain the many nation-states or to unite nationally, Manzoni favored unification. He supported the drive to bring all Italians under one government, and he wrote patriotic poems to help this cause. As a critic, he wrote fine essays on historical, linguistic, and religious topics. Concerned about the injustice and cruelty in the world, he also wrote a legal paper condemning the practice of torture.

Manzoni's major works of fiction brought him international recognition. The German writer Goethe praised the two tragedies: *Il Conte di Carmagnola (The Count of Carmagnola)* and *Adelchi*. With the publication of *I Promessi Sposi*, Manzoni took his place among the very best European writers. This historical novel proved him to be an author of outstanding literary skill.

I Promessi Sposi is set in the seventeenth century, when Spanish invaders were occupying Italian villages. The author portrays the lives of ordinary small-town people as they live through the normal events of their lives, experiencing happiness and misfortune. In describing the cruel separation of an engaged couple and their subsequent adventures, Manzoni presents a realistic picture of Italian life at this time. Some critics compare this novel to Cervantes' novel of Spain, *Don Quixote*.

Manzoni was a beloved celebrity at the time of his death. His poems and patriotic messages were well-known. The country gave him a magnificent funeral and even the great composer Verdi wrote a requiem in his honor.

Selection from Dante's Inferno *written in calligraphy*

Library (bibliotecha) *in Bologna, Italy*

La letteratura

Le attività

A **Indovina chi . . . (*Guess who . . .*)**

1. . . . criticized society in a poem.

_____

2. . . . encouraged patriotism.

_____

3. . . . advocated character development in dramas.

_____

4. . . . brought humor into plays.

_____

5. . . . portrayed society in a novel.

_____

6. . . . was sent into political exile.

_____

B **Fai corrispondere gli oggetti del gruppo *A* con quelli del gruppo *B*.**

A	B
1. _____ *I Promessi Sposi*	A. poem by Dante
2. _____ *Adelchi*	B. play by Goldoni
3. _____ *La Divina Commedia*	C. play by Manzoni
4. _____ *La Bottega del caffè*	D. novel by Manzoni
5. _____ *La Vita Nuova*	E. collection of poems by Dante

C ***Chi l'ha scritto?* Write the full name of the author of each work listed below.**

1. *Adelchi*

_____

2. *La Divina Commedia*

_____

3. *Il Bugiardo*

_____

4. *La Vita Nuova*

_____

5. *I Rusteghi*

_____

6. *I Promessi Sposi*

_____

D **Completa le analogie.**

1. humor: _____ = realism: Manzoni

2. Manzoni: compassion = Dante: _____

3. _____: Florence = Goldoni: Venice

4. poetry: Dante = _____: Goldoni

5. *Don Quixote:* Cervantes = _____: Manzoni

Fai corrispondere il nome all'illustrazione.

A   B

1. _____   A. Manzoni

2. _____   B. Dante

3. _____   C. Goldoni

F **Quale autore?** *(Which author or authors would most likely . . .)*

1. . . . encourage new playwrights?

_____

2. . . . support equal justice for all?

_____

3. . . . laugh at his own silly mistakes?

_____

4. . . . condemn cruelty to animals?

_____

5. . . . scold people who think too highly of themselves?

_____

6. . . . encourage each of us to do a good deed every day?

_____

G *È un brano lirico o realista?* **Label each passage with either "A" or "B."**
A indicates a lyrical style of writing or one with feeling.
B indicates a realistic or factual style.

1. _____ As the winter season approached, the air temperatures began to drop below 0 degrees Celsius. On this evening in late November, Laura was keeping warm near the fireplace. When she noticed the frost on the windowpane, she exclaimed loudly and ran to the window. As she reached out and touched the cold glass, she was dismayed. She felt a drop of water on her finger. How fast the warmth had turned to cold! How fast the ice had melted!

2. _____ As Jack Frost prepared to make his winter rounds, Laura started to think about mittens and extra blankets. On this evening she sat close to the fireplace, basking in the warm glow of the flames. As Jack glided his fingers over the shivering pane, Laura squealed with delight and ran to the window. As she reached out and greeted him, her joy turned to sorrow. An elf may not be held by a human being, not even for a second; otherwise he will die. At the very place were Laura's finger had touched Jack, there now remained only a tear.

H Completa ogni frase.

1. _____ gave up law practice.

2. _____ wrote a poem about life after death.

3. _____ was honored by Verdi.

4. _____ wrote in Latin as well as Italian.

5. _____ was called "Father of the Italian Comedy."

6. _____ became a national celebrity.

7. _____ wrote numerous plays.

8. _____ made religious and political enemies.

9. _____ wrote an historical novel.

I **Tocca a te!** **Choose one of the novels or plays mentioned in this chapter. Ask the librarian for help in finding the book and/or information about the plot. Look over carefully what you have found, and then, in your own words, retell the story to your classmates. You may wish to draw pictures on the board which relate to the story and the names of the main characters.**

Proverbio

" **Se non è vero, è ben trovato.**
Even if it's not true,
it makes a good story. "

Il meglio della narrativa contemporanea italiana,
in opere da leggere e da vivere.

Libri che hanno ispirato grandi film, vinto i più importanti premi letterari, che
si sono imposti nelle classifiche di vendita degli ultimi anni. Pagine che hanno
fatto sognare, parlare e riflettere l'Italia. Una collezione da avere e da amare.

**"GIRO DI VENTO" DI A. DE CARLO
DA LUNEDÌ 10 LUGLIO A SOLI € 7,90'**

Ogni lunedì in edicola
1. A. DE CARLO, Giro di vento _____ 10 luglio
2. M. MAZZANTINI, Non ti muovere _____ 17 luglio
3. A. CAMILLERI, Gli arancini di Montalbano _____ 24 luglio
4. A. PIPERNO, Con le peggiori intenzioni _____ 31 luglio
5. M. MAZZUCCO, Vita _____ 7 agosto
6. G. CAROFIGLIO, Il passato è una terra straniera _____ 14 agosto
7. A. SCURATI, Il sopravvissuto _____ 21 agosto
8. U. RICCARELLI, Il dolore perfetto _____ 28 agosto
9. A. PERISSINOTTO, Al mio giudice _____ 4 settembre

Vero Nord
di Bruce Henderson.
Corbaccio, 362
pagine, ill. in b.co e
nero, 18,60 euro.
Nel settembre del
1909 l'americano
Robert Peary, inge-
gnere civile, dichia-
ra di avere raggiun-
to il Polo cinque
mesi prima. E subi-
to il connazionale
Frederick Cook, un
medico generico

Diretto da Marco Albino Ferrari

IN EDICOLA

Libri
a cura di **Patrizia Rusconi**

La storia di una calligrafa, che della bella scrittura ha fatto un'arte e una preghiera

Con il romanzo della vita di sua nonna, docente all'università di Istanbul,
Yasmine Ghata **ha vinto il premio Edoardo Kihlgren Opera Prima 2006**

J The largest clipping on the page is a collection of contemporary Italian books. Can you find the answer to the following questions?

1. On which day of the week can you buy these books?

   _____

2. When can you buy the first book issued for this collection?

   _____

3. Which book can you buy on August 7th?

   _____

4. How much does each book cost?

   _____

5. When can you buy the last issue for this special collection?

   _____

K Look at the clippings and answer the following questions.

1. Can you find the word for "books"?

   _____

2. The word *vita* means life, what do you think *la mia vita* means?

   _____

3. In the book *La notte dei calligrafi,* the author talks about the life of a family member; which one?

   _____

4. How much does the book *Vero Nord* cost?

   _____

5. Can you guess what *Nord* means?

   _____

Symtalk

L Scrivi nello spazio la parola giusta in italiano. *(In the space, write the correct word in Italian.)*

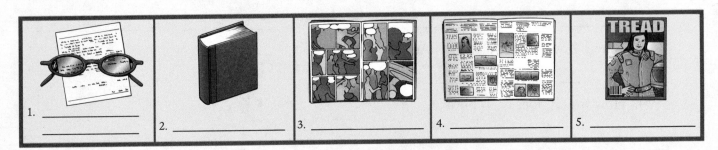

1. _____

2. _____

3. _____

4. _____

5. _____

M Dì le frasi, poi scrivile in italiano. *(Say the sentences, then write them in Italian.)*

1. _____

2. _____

3. _____

4. _____

1. _____
   _____
   _____
   _____
   _____

2. _____
   _____
   _____
   _____
   _____

3. _____
   _____
   _____
   _____
   _____

4. _____
   _____
   _____
   _____
   _____

Il cruciverba

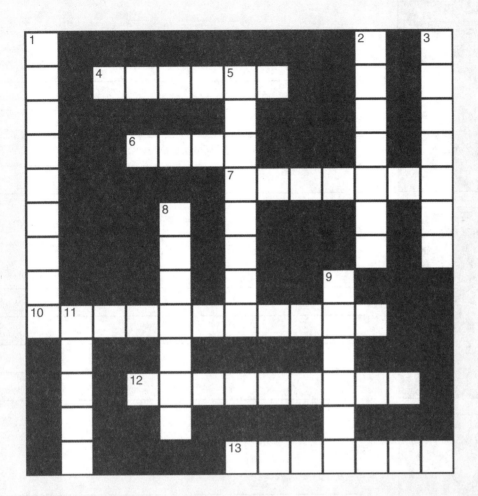

Orizzontale

4. city where Goldoni lived as a child
6. literary work with rhymes
7. he wrote in a realistic style
10. According to Dante, poetry is 10 percent
    ____.
12. poetic style used by Manzoni
13. city where Dante died

Verticale

1. Dante's surname
2. Father of the Italian Comedy
3. piece of music composed by Verdi in Manzoni's honor
5. *La Divina* ____
8. poetic style used by Dante
9. German author who praised Manzoni's work
11. literary work of fiction

Unit 18

Il tempo libero e la ricreazione
Leisure and Recreation

Il vocabolario

Dove vai?
Where are you going?

Vado alla partita.
I'm going to the game.

Vado al museo.
I'm going to the museum.

Vado alla festa.
I'm going to the party.

Vado alla spiaggia.
I'm going to the beach.

SOFIA:	**Dove vai stasera?**	Where are you going tonight?
MICHELE:	**Vado alla partita.**	I'm going to the game.
SOFIA:	**Anch'io!**	Me too!

❀✿❀✿❀

FRANCO:	**Che cosa fai oggi?**	What are you doing today?
CATERINA:	**Vado al museo . . . agli Uffizi.***	I'm going to the museum . . . to the Uffizi Museum.
FRANCO:	**Perchè?**	Why?
CATERINA:	**A vedere i quadri di Leonardo da Vinci.**	To see Da Vinci paintings.

*The Uffizi, the premier museum of Italian Renaissance art, is located in Florence.

A quali sport giochi?

What sports do you play?

Gioco a calcio.
I play soccer.

Gioco a pallavolo.
I play volleyball.

Gioco a tennis.
I play tennis.

Gioco a pallacanestro.
I play basketball.

Gioco a baseball.
I play baseball.

Gioco a football. I play football.

Che cosa ti piace fare?
What do you like to do?

Mi piace sciare.
I like skiing.

Mi piace leggere.
I like reading.

Mi piace ballare.
I like dancing.

Mi piace montare a cavallo.
I like horseback riding.

Mi piace nuotare.
I like swimming.

Mi piace andare in bicicletta.
I like biking.

MARCELLA:	C'è un picnic domani.	There's a picnic tomorrow.
GIANNI:	Dove?	Where?
MARCELLA:	Alla spiaggia. Vuoi venire con me?	At the beach. Do you want to come with me?
GIANNI:	Sì. Mi piace molto nuotare (Amo nuotare).	Yes. I love swimming.

❀✿❀✿❀

LUCIA:	Vai alla festa stasera?	Are you going to the party tonight?
MARTINO:	Certo. Ci sarà della musica, non è vero?	Of course! There'll be music, won't there?
LUCIA:	Sì. Amo ballare!	Yes. I love to dance!

Le attività

A Dove vai? Completa la frase in italiano. *(Where are you going? Complete each sentence in Italian, using the cues in parenthesis.)*

1. Vado alla _____. *(game)*

2. Vado a fare un _____. *(picnic)*

3. Vado al _____. *(museum)*

4. Vado alla _____. *(beach)*

5. Vado ad una _____. *(party)*

B Rispondi alle domande che hanno a che fare con i dialoghi di questo capitolo. *(The following questions are based on the dialogues presented in this unit. Review them before you choose the correct answers.)*

1. Quando è la partita?
   A. domani
   B. venerdì
   C. stasera
   D. dopo domani

2. Che cosa sono "gli Uffizi"?
   A. un cavallo
   B. un gioco
   C. i quadri di Leonardo da Vinci
   D. un museo

3. Chi è Leonardo da Vinci?
   A. un professore d'arte
   B. un artista italiano
   C. un direttore di un museo
   D. un attore italiano

4. Quando è il picnic?
   A. domani
   B. oggi
   C. dopo domani
   D. ieri

5. Dov'è il picnic?
   A. a Firenze
   B. agli Uffizi
   C. nel giardino
   D. alla spiaggia

C A quali sport giochi? Completa ogni frase in italiano. *(Which sports do you play? Complete each sentence in Italian.)*

1. Io gioco a _____.

2. Io gioco a _____.

3. Io gioco a _____.

4. Io gioco a _____.

5. Io gioco a _____.

D **Trova le parole.** *(Unscramble the words.)*

1. OGCIO _____

2. CINCIP _____

3. PIGASGIA _____

4. SATEF _____

5. USMOE _____

E **Che cosa ti piace fare? Completa ogni frase in italiano.** *(What do you like to do? Complete each sentence in Italian.)*

1. Mi piace _____ .

2. Mi piace _____ .

3. Mi piace _____ .

4. Mi piace _____ .

5. Mi piace _____ .

6. Mi piace _____.

7. Mi piace _____.

F **Completa il dialogo in italiano.** *(Complete the dialogue in Italian.)*

PATRIZIA: Dove (1.) _____ oggi?

MONICA: Io vado (2.) _____ spiaggia. Vuoi (3.)_____ con me?

PATRIZIA: (4.) _____. Amo la spiaggia.

MONICA: (5.) _____ io! Che cosa vuoi fare lì?

PATRIZIA: Mi piace giocare (6.) _____ pallavolo.

MONICA: Mi piace (7.) _____ nel mare *(sea)*.

G **Leggi il brano. Scegli la risposta giusta.** *(Read the passage. Choose the appropriate answers.)*

Claudia organizza una piccola festa *per* il suo compleanno. *Compie* dodici anni oggi. Invita *i suoi amici* Adolfo, Vittorio, Sabrina e Paolo. La festa *comincia* alle tre. Fa caldo e la spiaggia è molto *piacevole*. Ai suoi amici piace giocare a pallavolo e nuotare nel mare. *Dopo* la partita di pallavolo, i ragazzi avranno fame. Ci saranno dei panini, delle bibite, del gelato, e certamente, una torta. La festa del compleanno alla spiaggia *sarà* meravigliosa! Claudia è molto allegra oggi.

per	for
compie	she is turning
i suoi amici	her friends
comincia	starts
piacevole	pleasant
dopo	after
sarà	will be

1. Quanti anni ha Claudia oggi?
   A. 14
   B. 13
   C. 12
   D. 11

2. A che ora comincia la festa?
   A. alle cinque
   B. alle tre
   C. alle quattro
   D. alle due

3. Che tempo fa?
   A. Fa bel tempo.
   B. Nevica.
   C. Piove.
   D. Fa brutto tempo.

4. Ai ragazzi piace giocare a quale sport?
   A. pallacanestro
   B. baseball
   C. pallavolo
   D. calcio

5. Che cosa ci sarà da mangiare?
   A. una torta
   B. una spiaggia
   C. un ristorante
   D. una festa

H

Parliamo! Think of three places where you could go this weekend, such as a museum, a beach, a picnic. Your partner will ask you where you are going and you should answer appropriately. Then reverse the roles, using new places.

> **Modello:** A: Dove vai?
> B: Vado alla spiaggia.

I

Tocca a te! Try this word association game with a partner. Each of you writes a list of five nouns. You start by giving your partner your list. Time yourselves. Your partner will have one minute to say a word that is related to each noun, for example, *un libro, leggere; un museo, gli Uffizi.* If your partner finds five related words within one minute, he or she earns a reward. If not, then it's your turn: you trade roles and you try to guess five words in one minute. After you both take a turn, make new lists and repeat the activity.

Lingua viva!

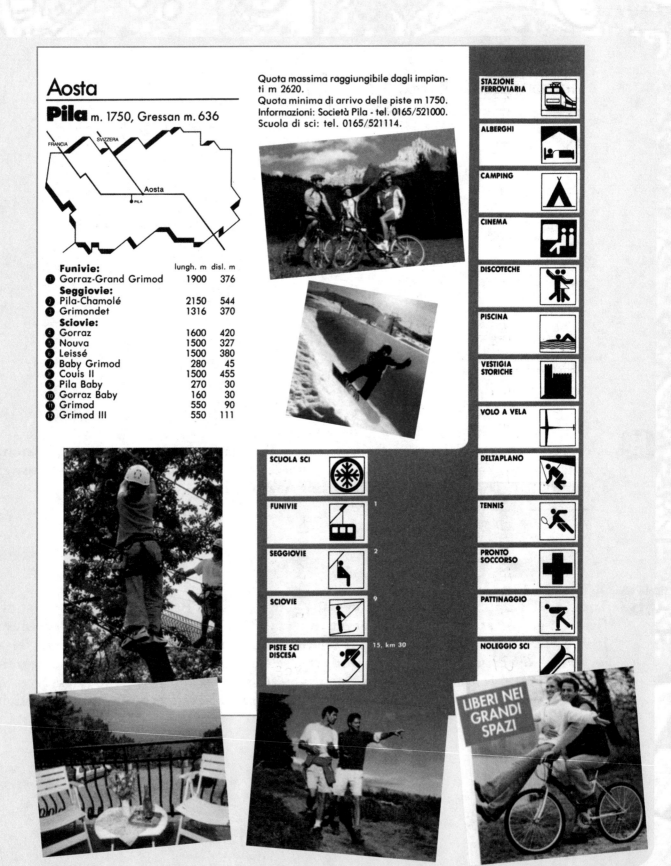

Aosta
Pila m. 1750, Gressan m. 636

FRANCIA SVIZZERA

Aosta
PILA

Funivie:	lungh. m	disl. m
❶ Gorraz-Grand Grimod	1900	376
Seggiovie:		
❷ Pila-Chamolé	2150	544
❸ Grimondet	1316	370
Sciovie:		
❹ Gorraz	1600	420
❺ Nouva	1500	327
❻ Leissé	1500	380
❼ Baby Grimod	280	45
❽ Couis II	1500	455
❾ Pila Baby	270	30
❿ Gorraz Baby	160	30
⓫ Grimod	550	90
⓬ Grimod III	550	111

Quota massima raggiungibile dagli impianti m 2620.
Quota minima di arrivo delle piste m 1750.
Informazioni: Società Pila - tel. 0165/521000.
Scuola di sci: tel. 0165/521114.

SCUOLA SCI

FUNIVIE 1

SEGGIOVIE 2

SCIOVIE 9

PISTE SCI DISCESA 15, km 30

STAZIONE FERROVIARIA

ALBERGHI

CAMPING

CINEMA

DISCOTECHE

PISCINA

VESTIGIA STORICHE

VOLO A VELA

DELTAPLANO

TENNIS

PRONTO SOCCORSO

PATTINAGGIO

NOLEGGIO SCI

LIBERI NEI GRANDI SPAZI

J Look at the clippings and answer the following questions.

1. Based on the symbols, what do you think *Stazione Ferroviaria* means?

   _____

2. This ski resort is on the border between Italy and which two other countries?

   _____

3. *Piste* means "slopes." How many kilometers of slopes can you find in this resort?

   _____

4. What is the altitude of this resort?

   _____

5. What is the name of this resort?

   _____

K Look at the symbols representing the activities offered at this resort. Can you guess what the following Italian words mean in English?

1. Discoteca

   _____

2. Piscina

   _____

3. Pronto soccorso

   _____

4. Pattinaggio

   _____

5. Vestigia storiche

   _____

Proverbio

> **Il riso fa buon sangue.** Laughter is the best medicine.

Symtalk

 L Scrivi nello spazio la parola giusta in italiano. *(In the space, write the correct word in Italian.)*

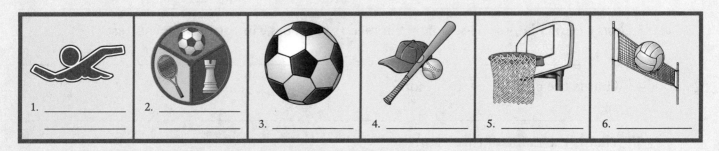

1. _____
   _____
2. _____
3. _____
4. _____
5. _____
6. _____

M Dì le frasi, poi scrivile in italiano. *(Say the sentences, then write them in Italian.)*

1.

   _____

2.

   _____

3.

   _____

4.

   _____

5.

_____

N **Fate le domande e rispondete. Poi, scrivete il dialogo.** _(With a partner, ask the question or give the answer. Then, write the dialogue.)_

1.

_____

No, _____

_____

2.

_____

No, _____

_____

3.

_____

No, _____

_____

4.

_____

No, _____

_____

Il cruciverba

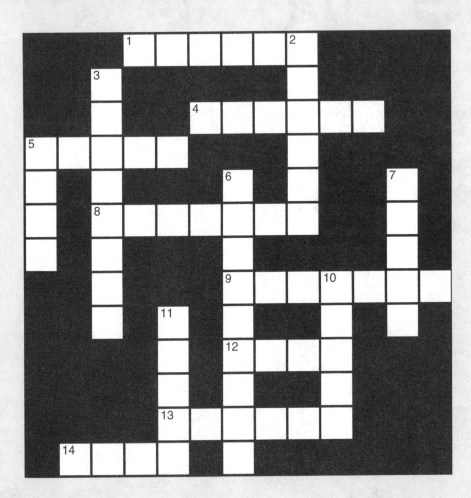

Orizzontale

1. game with a racquet and a ball
4. *un museo famoso a Firenze*
5. place of friends, music, games, and food
8. what you do at a dance
9. what you do with a book
12. *Io _____ agli Uffizi.*
13. game with a black and white ball
14. *_____ vai?*

Verticale

2. what you do with skis
3. game with a bat and a ball
5. *Che cosa ti piace _____?*
6. game with a net and a ball
7. *A quali _____ giochi?*
10. *Io _____ a tennis.*
11. *Mi _____ giocare a pallavolo.*

Unit **19**

Gli acquisti

Shopping

Il vocabolario

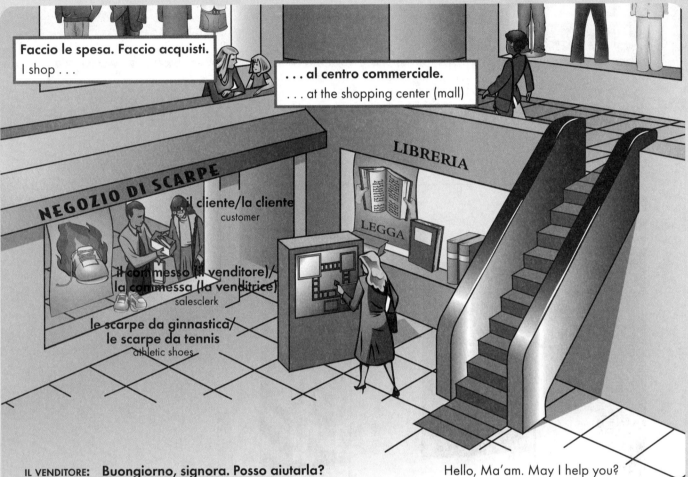

Faccio le spesa. Faccio acquisti.
I shop . . .

. . . al centro commerciale.
. . . at the shopping center (mall)

LIBRERIA

LEGGA

NEGOZIO DI SCARPE

il cliente/la cliente
customer

**il commesso (il venditore)/
la commessa (la venditrice)**
salesclerk

**le scarpe da ginnastica/
le scarpe da tennis**
athletic shoes

IL VENDITORE:	**Buongiorno, signora. Posso aiutarla?**	Hello, Ma'am. May I help you?
LA CLIENTE:	**No, grazie. Sto solo guardando.**	No, thanks. I'm just looking.

❀❀❀❀❀

IL VENDITORE:	**Buongiorno, signora. Posso aiutarla?**	Good morning, Ma'am. May I help you?
LA CLIENTE:	**Sì. Mi piacerebbe comprare un libro.**	Yes. I'd like to buy a book.
IL VENDITORE:	**Bene. Abbiamo una grande selezione.**	Fine. We have a large selection.

❀❀❀❀❀

DAVIDE:	**Dove vai?**	Where are you going?
PIA:	**Al centro commerciale.**	To the shopping center.
DAVIDE:	**Cosa compri?**	What are you going to buy?
PIA:	**Delle scarpe da ginnastica.**	Some athletic shoes.

The **euro** (€) is the currency of Italy and of most members of the European Union.

... al negozio.
... at the store

il cassiere/
la cassiera
cashier

il cliente/
la cliente
customer

i saldi/sono
in svendita
Sale

i soldi
money (bills or
paper money)

La cassa
cash register

gli spiccioli
(la moneta)
coins

un CD
compact disc, CD

LA CLIENTE:	Quanto costa questo CD?	How much is this compact disc?
IL CASSIERE:	Costa 15 Euro.	It costs 15 Euros.
LA CLIENTE:	È un pò caro!	That's a little expensive!
IL CASSIERE:	No, è a buon prezzo.	No, it's cheap.
LA CLIENTE:	Va bene. Lo compro. Ecco, signorina.	Okay. I'll buy it. There you are, Miss.
IL CASSIERE:	Molte grazie. Ecco il resto.	Thank you very much. Here's your change.

il venditore/
la venditrice
vendor

le pesche
peaches

i fagiolini
green or string beans

... al mercato.
... at the market.

| IL VENDITORE: | Qualcos'altro? | Anything else? |
| IL CLIENTE: | Euh ... tre pomodori, cinque pesche e alcuni fagiolini. Sì, va bene così. | Uhm ... three tomatoes, five peaches, and some string beans. Yes, that's all. |

Il vocabolario Extra

comprare	**costare**
to buy	to cost
Io compro	**costa**
I'm buying or I buy	it costs
fare acquisti/fare la spesa	**costano**
to shop (make purchases)	they cost

Le attività

A   Match the items for sale with the stores in which they can be found.

A	B
1. _____ le scarpe da tennis	A. market
2. _____ i fagiolini	B. shoe store
3. _____ i CD	C. furniture store
4. _____ un tavolo e delle sedie	D. stationery store
5. _____ le penne e i quaderni	E. music store

B   Usando le immagini, completa ogni frase. *(Using the picture cue, complete each sentence.)*

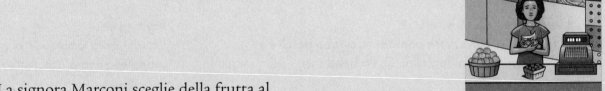

1. Io amo _____.

2. La signora Marconi sceglie della frutta al _____.

3. Io faccio la spesa al _____.

4. Ecco il _____, signore.

5. Il CD è a buon prezzo. _____ quindici euro.

C **Scegli l'espressione.** *(Choose the expression from the following list that completes each sentence correctly.)*

a buon prezzo   euro   un negozio   il   comprare

Pietro va ad (1.) _____ di musica . Vuole (2.) _____ un CD di musica classica. C'è un CD di Pavarotti. Costa 15 (3.) _____. Non è caro. È (4.) _____. Pietro compra (5.) _____ CD.

D Scegli la risposta corretta. *(Choose the correct answers.)*

1. Se vedi il segno *saldi,* come pensi che sia il prezzo?
   A. a buon prezzo
   B. i soldi
   C. caro
   D. gli spiccioli

2. How do you reply if the cashier says *"Costa 10 euro"*?
   A. Ecco.
   B. Quanto costa?
   C. Dov'è il mercato?
   D. Grazie, va bene così.

3. What do you get back if you give the cashier too much money?
   A. una cassa
   B. un centro commerciale
   C. i soldi
   D. il resto

4. Who helps you find what you need?
   A. le pesche
   B. il venditore
   C. il cassiere
   D. il cliente

5. What do you say if you don't need the salesclerk's help right now?
   A. Posso aiutarla?
   B. È un pò caro!
   C. Sto solo guardando, grazie.
   D. Qualcos'altro?

E Scrivi in inglese. *(Write the English for the following.)*

1. Compro delle scarpe da tennis.

   _____

2. Tu compri sette pesche.

   _____

3. Lei compra un CD. (**Hint:** *Lei* refers to *la cliente.*)

   _____

F Scegli la risposta corretta per ogni domanda. *(Choose the correct answer for each question.)*

1. Basta così?
   A. No, è a buon prezzo.
   B. No, alcune pesche, per favore.
   C. Vado al mercato.
   D. Sto solo guardando.

2. Perché vai al negozio?
   A. Il CD costa quindici euro.
   B. Non ho molti soldi.
   C. Mi piacerebbe comprare un libro.
   D. Il cliente parla con il venditore.

3. Le scarpe da ginnastica sono a buon prezzo?
   A. Sì, ho i soldi.
   B. No, è il venditore.
   C. Sì, basta così.
   D. No, sono care.

4. Quanto costa il CD?
   A. Costa 15 euro.
   B. La cassa è qui.
   C. No, è caro.
   D. È al centro commerciale.

5. Che cosa compri?
   A. al mercato
   B. alla cassa
   C. i pomodori
   D. gli spiccioli

G **Completa la conversazione.** *Alfonso is shopping in a clothing store. Complete his conversation with the sales clerk.*

IL VENDITORE: Buongiorno, signore. Posso (1.) _____ ?

ALFONSO: Sto solo (2.) _____ .

IL VENDITORE: Abbiamo dei saldi. Tutto è (3.) _____ : le camicie, i pantaloni, i cappotti e le scarpe.

ALFONSO: Grazie, signore. Allora, quanto (4.) _____ questi pantaloni blu?

IL VENDITORE: Costano trenta euro.

ALFONSO: Sono un pò (5.) _____ . Non posso *(I can't)* comprare i pantaloni. Non ho trenta euro.

H **Parliamo! Think of three things you would like to buy (for example, a notebook, a shirt, a sandwich). You need to know the price of each item. Ask your partner how much each one costs *Quanto costa . . . ?* He/she should tell you a specific price. Then react to the price by saying: *È a buon prezzo* or *È caro* or *Va bene.***

I **Tocca a te! You and your partner are going to play store today. To start, one of you is the customer and the other is the salesclerk. The salesclerk greets the customer and offers help. The customer says that he/she wants to buy a certain item. The salesclerk mentions the large selection of that item. The customer asks how much one costs. The clerk helps with the purchase, thanks the customer and says good-bye. Use real items such as a *una riga, un quaderno, un CD, un maglione, un libro, una penna, una mela* and use imaginary money and a cash register. Make a little sign to place in front of you on the desk for the dialogue activity, e.g., *Il negozio di Filippo* or *il mercato di Maria.* Then trade roles.**

Look at the clippings and answer the following questions.

1. Look at the ad selling socks, can you guess what the following words mean in English?

    A. Comfort Estremo _____

    B. Medio _____

    C. Massimo _____

2. Look at the ad for purses. How many stores sell this product?

    _____

3. Can you find the Italian word for purses?

    _____

4. *Valigia* means "suitcase." Can you guess what *accessori* means?

    _____

5. Find the Italian word for "how to buy"? Hint: The English word "acquire" comes from the same Latin root.

    _____

6. *Vende* is the opposite of "to buy." Can you guess its English meaning?

    _____

7. This store sells and buys Rolex; based on this famous brand's name can you guess what the word orologi means?

    _____

8. This ad also mentions two other products sold in this store; what are they?

    _____

9. What do you think *Servizio Clienti* means in English?

    _____

Proverbio

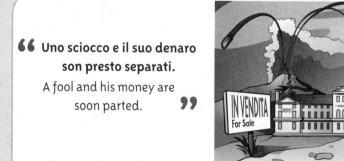

" Uno sciocco e il suo denaro
   son presto separati.
   A fool and his money are
   soon parted. "

Symtalk

K Scrivi nello spazio la parola giusta in italiano. *(In the space, write the correct word in Italian.)*

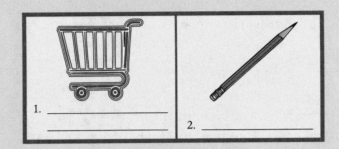

1. _____

2. _____

L Dì le frasi, poi scrivile in italiano. *(Say the sentences, then write them in Italian.)*

1.

2.

3.

4.

5.

Fate le domande e rispondete. Poi, scrivete il dialogo. *(With a partner, ask the question or give the answer. Then, write the dialogue.)*

1.

_____   _____.

2.

_____   _____.

3.

_____   _____.

4.

_____   _____.

5.

_____   _____.

Il cruciverba

Orizzontale

1. female salesclerk
5. where fresh vegetables are sold
8. cash register
10. expensive, costly, dear
11. *un* ____: a long, thin green vegetable (singular)
13. sporty *scarpe*
14. ____ *aiutarla?*

Verticale

2. ____ *vai?* (to) where, one word
3. *il* ____: compact disc
4. That's all.
6. a fuzzy sweet fruit
7. *Sto solo* ____.
8. female customer
9. what you pay your bill with
12. *Qualcos'* ____?

Unit 20

Viaggiare e il trasporto
Travel and Transportation

Il vocabolario

Come viaggi?
How do you travel?

Viaggio in aereo.
I travel by plane.

Viaggio in macchina.
I travel by car.

Viaggio in autobus.
I travel by bus.

Viaggio in nave.
I travel by ship.

Viaggio in treno.
I travel by train.

Vocabolario extra

volare	to fly
Io volo	I fly.
viaggiare	to travel
Dove si trova?/Dov'è?	Where is? How can I get to . . .?

L'automobile and *l'auto* are two other words for car.

all'aeroporto
at the airport

l'agente
clerk, agent

il passaporto
passport

la valigia
suitcase

**il viaggiatore/
la viaggiatrice**
traveler

lo sportello
ticket counter

IMPIEGATA:	Il suo passaporto, signore?	Your passport, Sir?
VIAGGIATORE:	È nella mia valigia, signorina.	It's in my suitcase, Miss.
IMPIEGATA:	Ma deve averlo in mano . . . e specialmente al controllo quando arriva.	But you must have it in hand . . . and especially at passport control upon arrival.
VIAGGIATORE:	Va bene. Aspetti, per favore. Eccolo! E dove ci imbarchiamo?	Okay. Wait, please. Here it is! And where do we board?
IMPIEGATA:	All'uscita d'imbarco 25, a destra. Buon viaggio!	At gate 25, on your right. Have a good trip!

l'impiegato/
l'impiegata
clerk

il biglietto
ticket

il viaggiatore/
la viaggiatrice
traveler

l'orario
schedule

VIAGGIATRICE:	**A che ora parte il prossimo treno per Roma, signore?**	At what time does the next train for Rome leave, Sir?
IMPIEGATO:	**A mezzogiorno, signora. Ecco l'orario.**	At noon, Ma'am. Here's the schedule.
VIAGGIATRICE:	**Bene, allora mi piacerebbe comprare un biglietto di andata e ritorno in seconda classe.**	Good, then I'd like to buy a round-trip ticket in second class.
IMPIEGATO:	**Ecco il biglietto. Sono 75 Euro.**	Here's the ticket. It's 75 euros.

nella via
on the street

l'autobus
bus

IL SIGNOR SPINI:	**Mi scusi signora . . . dove si trova l'Hotel Ritz?**	Excuse me Ma'am . . . how do I get to the Ritz Hotel?
LA SIGNORA FIORE:	**Prenda l'autobus numero 7 e scenda all'ufficio postale. L'albergo è a sinistra.**	Take bus number 7 and get off at the post office. The hotel is on the left.
IL SIGNOR SPINI:	**Grazie, signora.**	
LA SIGNORA FIORE:	**Prego, signore.**	

Lei is the formal pronoun that means **you**. Use it together with the "lei" verb forms to talk to an adult whom you don't know well.

Le attività

A Match the Italian with the English.

A		B	
1. _____	Aspetti.	A.	a round-trip ticket
2. _____	Mi piacerebbe	B.	on the right
3. _____	a sinistra	C.	Where do we board?
4. _____	Scenda all'ufficio postale.	D.	Here's the schedule.
5. _____	Dove ci imbarchiamo?	E.	Get off at the post office.
6. _____	Prenda l'autous.	F.	You must have it in hand.
7. _____	un biglietto di andata e ritorno	G.	Wait.
8. _____	Deve averlo.	H.	I would like
9. _____	Ecco l'orario.	I.	Take the bus.
10. _____	a destra	J.	on the left

B Come viaggi? Completa ogni frase in italiano. (*How do you travel? Complete each sentence in Italian.*)

1. Io viaggio _____.

2. Io viaggio _____.

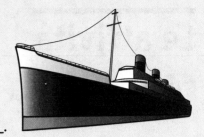

3. Io viaggio _____.

4. Io viaggio _____.

5. Io viaggio _____.

C Scegli le risposte giuste. *(Choose the correct answers.)*

1. Where do you go to take a train?
   A. all'aeroporto
   B. al controllo dei passaporti
   C. alla stazione
   D. alla via

2. What do you ask if you want directions to the train station?
   A. Dove ci imbarchiamo?
   B. Dove si trova la stazione?
   C. A che ora parte il treno?
   D. Come posso aiutarla?

3. What do you look at to find the times when trains, buses, and planes arrive and leave?
   A. un orario
   B. uno sportello
   C. un passaporto
   D. una valigia

4. What do you say when you want to buy a ticket?
   A. Ecco il mio passaporto.
   B. Mi piacerebbe comprare un biglietto.
   C. Dove vai?
   D. Dove si trova l'ufficio postale?

5. If you don't want a first-class ticket, what do you say?
   A. un biglietto di andata e ritorno
   B. la stazione
   C. l'autobus numero 2
   D. seconda classe

D Trova le parole. *(Unscramble the words.)*

1. TELOSPLOR _____

2. ROIRAO _____

3. GLEBITOIT _____

4. IVAROGIGATE _____

5. PAROTASOSP _____

Leggi il brano. Rispondi alle domande. *(Read the passage. Answer the questions.)*

Fa bel tempo oggi. Michela e Angela fanno un viaggio in treno. Sono *davanti allo* sportello della stazione. Michela compra due biglietti per Bologna. I nonni di Michela abitano a Bologna. Le ragazze *aspettano* il treno al *binario* numero quattro. Il treno arriva alla stazione alle quattordici. Le ragazze salgono sul treno. Angela sceglie *un posto accanto al finestrino*. Le amiche parlano della loro visita a Bologna. A Bologna, le ragazze vanno in autobus alla casa dei nonni.

davanti a	in front of
aspettano	they wait for
binario	railroad track
un posto	a seat
accanto a	next to
finestrino	window

1. Dove sono Michela e Angela?
   A. all'aeroporto
   B. in autobus
   C. in taxi
   D. alla stazione

2. Dove vanno le ragazze?
   A. a Roma
   B. a Bologna
   C. ad Amalfi
   D. a Cortona

3. Quanti biglietti compra Michela?
   A. due
   B. uno
   C. quattordici
   D. quattro

4. Dov'è il treno?
   A. accanto alla finestra
   B. davanti allo sportello
   C. al binario numero quattro
   D. nelle valige

5. Come vanno dalla *(from)* stazione alla *(to)* casa dei nonni?
   A. in treno
   B. in autobus
   C. in macchina
   D. in nave

F **Completa le analogie.**

1. impiegato: _____ = viaggiatore: viaggiatrice

2. aereo: aeroporto = treno: _____

3. nave: oceano = autobus: _____

4. impiegato: _____ = professore: scrivania

5. uno: due = primo: _____

G **Parliamo!** Look at the pictures of a bus, an airplane, a car, a ship, and a train. Ask your speaking partner what each one is *(Che cos'è?)*. He/she will answer. Then ask him/her *Come viaggi?* as you point to a specific picture and he/she will answer again.

H **Tocca a te!** With a partner, act out the last dialogue, *Nella via*. One of you will be *Il signor Spini* and the other *La signora Fiore*. This time, however, Il signor Spini wants to go to another destination within the city. He will substitute another name for L'Hotel Ritz (i.e. *l'albergo Excelsior, il museo del Vaticano, lo zoo*). La signora Fiore will recommend a different bus number. She will finish giving directions by saying that the place is on the right. Don't forget to say "Thank you" and "You're welcome!"

Proverbio

“ Paese che vai,
usanza che trovi.
como vieres.

The country you visit,
the customs you find.
(When in Rome, do as
the Romans do.) ”

Lingua viva!

Ottobre: Operazione VISIBILITA' OK!

E il controllo dell'impianto di illuminazione e spazzole tergi è GRATIS.

L'officina Bosch Car Service si prende cura della mia auto di ogni marca e modello. Professionalità, competenza e cortesia garantiti in tutta Italia.

 Bosch Car Service: tutto con qualità e convenienza.

BOSCH Service

SU SPAZZOLE E LAMPADINE
SCONTO 30%

SPECIALE CAMERETTE
Scegli il tuo REGALO

MINI MOTO R3 - 49cc

MOUNTAIN BIKE 24"

PIANO DELLA MOBILITA': UN PROGETTO DI GRANDE RESPIRO

BO₂

C'È POSTO PER TE [Cambia l'auto col bus]

I parcheggi di interscambio P+bus [gratuiti per utenti ATC] sono raggiungibili anche quando sono in vigore le limitazioni al traffico per la qualità dell'aria

→TANARI [via Tanari]
tutti i giorni 24 ore su 24
P+bici: parcheggio gratuito per chi deposita la bici e la usa dopo aver parcheggiato l'auto
P+taxi: parcheggio gratuito per utenti taxi
BUS: 18, navette A e B

ESPORRE IL TAGLIAND(SU_ CRUSCOTTO BEN VISIBILE DALL'ESTERI

VIA MARTIRI LIBERTA' (

No. 2532 10:44 01.08.(

Fine Sosta

11:34

01.08.06

EUR 0.50

COMUNE DI CHATILLO(

CO.GE.CO Park
Via Fantoni 2 G
BERGAMO

tsp ITALIA SRL BERGAMO

tsp ITALIA SRL B

I   **Look at the clippings and answer the following questions.**

    1. Bosch Service is an *officina;* what do you think that means in English?

    _____

    2. Find the Italian word for "car."

    _____

    3. Find the Italian words for "quality and convenience."

    _____

    4. What do you think *SCONTO* means?

    _____

    5. In which month can you get *30% SCONTO*?

    _____

J   **One of these clippings is an ad asking people to park their car and take another mode of transportation to go to work. Find that clipping and answer the following questions:**

    1. *Cambia* means exchange; what do you think *"Cambia l'auto con il bus"* means?

    _____

    2. *P+bus* means park and take the bus; can you guess what *P+bici* means?

    _____

    3. There is a third *P+* option. Find it.

    _____

    4. What is the number of the bus leaving from this parking lot?

    _____

    5. The word *Navette* means shuttle; how many shuttle options are offered?

    _____

Symtalk

K Scrivi nello spazio la parola giusta in italiano. *(In the space, write the correct word in Italian.)*

1._____
_____

2._____

3._____

4._____

L Dì le frasi, poi scrivile in italiano. *(Say the sentences, then write them in Italian.)*

1._____

2._____

3._____

4._____

Viaggiare e il trasporto

5. _____

M **Scrivi una descrizione di ogni scena in italiano.** *(Write a description of each scene in Italian.)*

1. _____
_____
_____
_____
_____

2. _____
_____
_____
_____
_____

3. _____
_____
_____
_____
_____

4. _____
_____
_____
_____
_____

Il cruciverba

Orizzontale

1. (Get off) _____ *all'ufficio postale.*
4. *Il* _____: what you show at passport control
5. *Dove ci* _____? (Where do we board?)
9. *Il treno* _____ *a mezzogiorno.*
12. means of traveling on water
13. female traveler
14. They wait.

Verticale

2. opposite of *sinistra*
3. *Il prossimo treno* _____ *Napoli parte alle 12.*
5. *Io viaggio* _____ *treno.*
6. _____ *viaggio!* (Have a good trip!)
7. female clerk
8. street
10. *Un biglietto di andata e* _____.
11. where